What people are saying about
Look Out Above!

Look Out Above*! is a brilliantly written and highly entertaining guide to excelling in today's work environment. It combines real life experiences and valuable insights with a unique sense of humor. LOA! is a fabulous resource for young and old alike.* LILI DUNN, PRESIDENT, BELL PARTNERS

Bob and Nick have drawn on decades of experience and wisdom to create an entertaining and practical field guide to career success. It's a must read for those who want to be more effective at any stage of life. STEPHEN MILLER, FORMER VICE CHAIRMAN AND EXECUTIVE VICE PRESIDENT, BILTMORE ESTATE, ASHEVILLE, NC

A straightforward and humorous insight into the fundamental (and often overlooked) soft skills that are critical for growth and success in today's business environment—yet not widely taught in Business School. I wish I could have read Look Out Above*! five years ago.* ERIC RASMUSSEN, REGIONAL DIRECTOR, JOHNSON DEVELOPMENT ASSOCIATES (YOUNG PROFESSIONAL)

Many Americans haven't read a book since high school. If you're looking to buy a book that you're probably not going to read, let it be Look Out Above*! Or, if you prefer not to listen, try the audio version.* NICK SLATER, AUTHOR (YOUNG PROFESSIONAL)

I'm impressed with the vast amount of practical and proven information in these pages. I know they can boost the career of a young executive because I saw them work for so many (including one of the authors). If I were starting my career I would have a dogeared copy of Look Out Above*! at my side and my MBA on the wall.* DICK MICHAUX, FORMER CEO, AVALONBAY COMMUNITIES, INC.

Look Out Above*! is a captivating book that gives clear guidance about how to make meaningful contributions at work, particularly for those who are early on in their careers. Success is increasingly dependent on excellent communication and critical thinking skills, as well as how to collaborate with others. This book gives great insights on how to develop these skills and how to become an influencer without authority. If you're open to learning practical skills, engage with this book.* GWYNETH COTE, PRESIDENT AMERICAS, URBAN LAND INSTITUTE

D1516645

You will find more good sense in a single page of Look Out Above! *than in most workplace guides in their entirety, not to mention most workplaces.*
FRED KAMENY, LAWYER AND EDITOR

The Slaters provide a terrific multigenerational perspective on how young professionals can prepare for success. Much like a parent and sibling who we would love to have help guide us in our career journeys, the Slaters link together advice with personal stories in a practical and applied approach. The soft skills they emphasize and provide developmental advice around in Look Out Above!—*from communications, to successful collaboration, to critical thinking—are the exact skills that employers most value, but struggle to find and develop in their talent pools.* RUSS MORGAN, SR. ASSOCIATE DEAN, DUKE UNIVERSITY FUQUA SCHOOL OF BUSINESS

Oh, but that I could walk and talk with those Slater boys. They have mastered my methods, and more. ARISTOTLE, PHILOSOPHER AND EDUCATOR

Look Out Above! *is packed with actionable advice and down-to-earth examples of how to distinguish oneself in the workplace. Those who wish to excel at work would be wise to read it twice.* KRIS BENNETT, ENTREPRENEUR AND PODCAST HOST (YOUNG PROFESSIONAL)

Bob and Nick have written what I believe will become a must-read business classic. Should be required reading for the up-and-coming. Look Out Above! *is filled with realistic, actionable guidance for distinguishing oneself in the workplace and rising through the ranks. Add to that, Bob and Nick's easy humor and personal stories will keep you as entertained as you are informed.* JEFF REMSBURG, EDITOR, INVESTORPLACE DIGEST (YOUNG PROFESSIONAL)

With Look Out Above! *Bob and Nick Slater have put together a compendium of helpful tips for a successful career in any field or industry. Everything you wanted to know that you didn't learn in business school is here—from clear business writing and giving powerful presentations to managing relationships with bosses and colleagues. Sprinkled with humor and personal anecdotes,* Look Out Above! *is packed with wisdom and practical guidance for all young professionals.* CHARLENE ROTHKOPT, FORMER EVP OF HUMAN RESOURCES, MARRIOTT INTERNATIONAL

Not since Boethius' Consolation of Philosophy *have I encountered such a worthy tome. The lash of my whip shall fall across the pitiful shoulders of fools who dare not read it.* IGNATIUS J. REILLY

Look Out Above!

Look Out Above!

The Young Professional's Guide to Success

Bob & Nick Slater

Bulldog Ventures Media, LLC | Chapel Hill, North Carolina

ISBN: 978-1-7330147-0-0

Library of Congress Control Number: 2019940994

Printed by Versa Press, Inc. in the United States of America

Design and production by BW&A Books, Inc.
Cover design by Jules Epstein
Caricatures by JP Trostle

Bulldog Ventures Media, LLC

www.lookoutabove.com

Look Out Above!
is dedicated to you,
the young professional

Contents

Conventions

To make the book as readable as possible we adopted the following conventions:

1. When referring to your manager or anyone else, we will not always say "he or she" or "him or her." We tried this and found it to be tedious. We chose to use "he" or "him" and "she" or "her" randomly throughout the book (with an occasional "he or she" or "him or her" thrown in). When we do so we mean the person referenced, no matter what sex they are. We trust you understand and will give us the benefit of the doubt.

2. We use "company," "organization," and "firm" interchangeably. We know some of you work for non-profits or the government. We're writing for you, too. Please consider yourself included when we use these terms.

3. We use "manager" and "supervisor" and "boss" interchangeably. Different organizations use different terms. No change of meaning is intended when we use one of these words versus another.

4. We use contractions and fragments liberally. We recognize that when a document needs a more formal tone, such as when writing to your manager, clients, or prospective clients, these should be used sparingly or not at all. Since we are writing informally to new friends, we use contractions and fragments to be conversational.

5. Notes and sources are in the back of the book. If you want the source of a study, statistic, or quote, you'll find it here, along with occasional commentary. We think you'll find this information more interesting than it sounds, and worth a look.

Start Here!

*"That is a good book which is opened with expectation,
and closed with delight and profit."*

AMOS BRONSON ALCOTT, TEACHER AND WRITER

The LOA! Way

Contribute
Commit, Connect, Create Value

Write
Be Clear, Be Concise, Be Correct

Present
*Master the Structure, Enhance with Graphics,
Stand and Deliver*

Pitch
Prepare, Sell, Close

Lead
*Unify Your Team, Develop Their Skills,
Achieve Team Goals*

Advocate
*Understand the Game, Advocate for Yourself,
Advocate for Others*

Transform
Become Confident, Dynamic, Heroic!

Start Here

You are bright, talented, and likely credentialed from a college or university. As you may have noticed, however, academic success has a short shelf life in the real world. Testing well, attending a good school, and getting great grades no longer matter. What matters now is accomplishment, which, in turn, depends on your ability to contribute, write, present, pitch ideas, lead, and advocate in the manner valued in the workplace.

Look Out Above! is your guide for developing these critical workplace skills. In a crowded market, we've not seen anything like it. The value here is threefold:

1. Practical, proven, real-world content
2. A focused, less-is-more approach
3. Dual perspectives from a young professional and a seasoned executive

We distill these workplace skills to their essence, translate them to real-world applications not taught in undergraduate and graduate business schools or in company training, and present them in one book. Each chapter does the job of an entire book to provide you with the greatest benefit in the least amount of time.

The guidance and insight provided here are intended for those who are in the first five or so years of their working life after completing college or graduate school. Whether you're working at a for-profit, a non-profit, or in government, and whether you're working for others or running your own business, our objective is to help you be different—and better: to stand out while fitting in. The skills you hone here will serve you throughout your career, wherever you go, and whatever you do.

Nick

I'm an entrepreneur with a law degree who practiced law for about 20 minutes and is now seeking to make it in the business world. If you're a young professional in the working world my father and I created this book for you.

I'm here to see that *Look Out Above!* speaks to you as a young professional. I helped shape its content to ensure that it provides what we need for where we are now. I gave a young person's perspective to my co-author, and argued with him when we disagreed, well-intentioned as he is. You've been spared teachings from *The Godfather*, references to outdated movies, books, and songs, and more musings of arcane ancient philosophers. While Aristotle, Plato, and Socrates drop in on occasion, their role is limited and on point.

Consider me a kindred spirit on your journey to succeed in the working world. More so than our parents, or their parents, you and I had a structured upbringing with a steady stream of activities designed to ensure our development and entry into a good college. We now find ourselves in a work environment that is increasingly unstructured and insecure. It requires and rewards a different set of skills than we were taught. Career paths aren't as clearly defined, and simply showing up and doing what we're told isn't enough. Our challenge is to be creative, take initiative, and have the courage to take risks.

We also bring a different perspective to our work. Whether following a corporate path or trying to earn a living doing our own thing, we seem more determined than those who came before us to create a life first and a career second. Many of us fight the cultural imperative to be dissatisfied with who and where we are and to always be striving for more. Without minimizing the importance of money, and while recognizing the reality of workplace competition, we bring a more balanced perspective about the role of work in our lives.

My goal, and perhaps yours, is not so much to fashion a career to boast about or to satisfy the expectations of others, but to create a life that reflects my values, contributes to the greater good, and satisfies. Without minimizing the importance of money, and while work is a meaningful part of that life, we are so much more than our work. Bosses will come and go, while other people and priorities in our lives will, hopefully, remain constants.

Bob

As a former trial lawyer with 25 years of business experience, I've helped build two nationwide real estate companies, one public and one private. I enjoy teaching and mentoring young people, which is why Nick and I created Look Out Above!

I'm here to be the voice of experience, and to help you bridge the gap between a formal education and a practical one. I've spent most of my working life in the corporate worlds of law and real estate, at a high level, with some success. When I switched from law to real estate, my first day on the job was in San Diego at a multi-day company conference. My peers from cities across the country were MBA graduates, and many talked excitedly about the deals they had going. I had no MBA degree, no deals, and no understanding of much of what was said. Everyone was so credentialed and confident. It seemed like a gathering of the best and brightest, other than me. Fast forward ten years, and I was one of the few still with the company, and had climbed the corporate ladder to a considerable height. That happened by applying the lessons offered to you here.

For over ten years now I've taught some of these lessons to undergrads and MBA students at the University of North Carolina's Kenan-Flagler School of Business and, starting recently, MBA students at Duke University's Fuqua School of Business. This book was conceived to help young people (such as my three sons) advance in their professional lives. That one of my sons has been my partner in this has been great fun. Criticize the content as you wish, but rest assured it's far better thanks to Nick.

Please consider me a proxy for your boss (or boss's boss), who like me may be a baby boomer. Although we're retiring in record numbers every day, departing with institutional knowledge and practical know-how, there will be plenty of us around for years to come. Regardless of age, any advancement of yours will likely be reviewed and blessed, or not, by a boss who thinks like I do. In an environment where it's easier than ever to outsource, and where work is increasingly robotized, it's imperative that you learn what is expected and valued in the workplace.

How to Get the Most from *Look Out Above!*

This is a "how-to" book more than an advice or motivational book. Likely you're not lacking for advice, and you're already motivated. The skills taught in *Look Out Above!* are known as soft skills: communicating orally and in

writing, working with others, making decisions, solving problems, thinking critically. These skills are valued across industries and are said to account for 85% of success in business. Contributing, leading, and advocating are more judgment-oriented skills, while writing, presenting, and pitching have more rules around them. But each skill allows for creativity, and for you to apply your unique perspective and style.

"But I already have these skills," you may protest. Maybe, but unlikely. In a recent Deloitte study, more than 70% of almost 8,000 college-educated millennials responded that their current organization isn't making "full use" of their skills. That's a lot of companies under-utilizing expensive human capital. Could this disconnect be because their skills aren't as developed—or as useful to their employer—as these young professionals think? In fairness, it's hard to imagine where, how, or from whom you would have learned these skills to the extent that today's working world demands. Bright students from leading schools as well as seasoned executives seemingly don't know or haven't mastered the material that follows.

Most people read zero business-related books each year. Zero is a small market! Undaunted, we proceed anyway, hoping you'll recognize the need to develop the skills presented in *Look Out Above!* While intended for those relatively new to the working world, what follows is not beginner content. As you will soon see and hopefully agree, there's a depth of content borne of experience that would benefit those outside our target audience. Nonetheless, we marketed this book to young professionals for a reason—there's a sense of urgency for you to develop these skills. As automation and outsourcing strip away mindless tasks, employers are demanding more, sooner. They want fast learners with exceptional soft skills who can interact effectively with clients to solve their problems. Master this material now to gain the most leverage from it.

Consider how many ideas which, if you implemented them, would make *Look Out Above!* a worthwhile read. Ten? Five? Three? What if you took just one action that you otherwise would not have taken, and that you apply and benefit from for the rest of your career? For these ideas to have value, you must experiment with and apply them. *Look Out Above!* is not meant to be read once and left to collect dust on a shelf or be deleted from your device. We hope you'll dog-ear the pages, highlight the text, and make notes in the margins to add your ideas and lessons learned. Refer to it often, not only when specific projects and presentations arise, but to develop an intentional approach to work and leadership. Only by doing so will you learn which ideas work best for you.

What we teach is gettable, and doable. While natural ability is not irrelevant, and while work ethic is relevant, the *Look Out Above!* skills are learned skills.

You'll improve and perfect them with practice. And while each generation brings its own unique approach to work and the workplace, we believe the content is timeless.

Are you ready for a practical business education not offered in college or grad school? Ready to learn what actions to take to set yourself apart? Ready to increase your effectiveness, and ultimately your career satisfaction? If so, as our favorite literary protagonist Ignatius J. Reilly would say, "Clear your valve, grab a Big Chief tablet, open a frosty Dr. Nut, and pay heed."

In other words, let's get started!

Bob Slater and Nick Slater
Chapel Hill, North Carolina

Contribute!

CHAPTER ONE

"Work hard, trust in God, and keep your bowels open."

BERYL MARKHAM, AVIATION PIONEER

Contribute

Contributing in the workplace is giving something of value—your time and talent—for a common purpose. It means helping to change your company for the better. If you work for someone else, contributing matters because doing so promotes job security and advancement. If you work for yourself, contributing matters because your economic survival depends on it. If you don't make it happen, it doesn't happen.

We know an executive at a leading public company who urges young professionals, "Do your job, keep your job." This succinct advice, restated, means that to succeed, focus on your performance, and not on the performance of others, the travel reimbursement policy, the dress code, or anything else. Why do people lose their jobs? Usually because:

- They don't adequately perform their job.
- Their position is eliminated because of downsizing.
- Their position is eliminated due to an internal restructure, merger, or acquisition.

Or, in the Animal House tradition, they commit "individual acts of perversion so profound and disgusting that decorum prohibits listing them here."

Contributing is your best job security. If you master your job—and grow with it—you'll control what you can. To the greatest extent possible, you'll give yourself the opportunity to stay, or to leave if and when you want.

Contributing is also required for advancement. Most hierarchical companies use a pyramid structure: more worker bees than managers, more managers than regional managers, more regional managers than VPs. The next step up is obvious, and available only to a smaller group. Companies with a flatter structure use fewer or no managers.

> *When touring an insurance company's headquarters, I was told that a person's level could be gleaned by his or her standard-issue furniture package, down to the shape of the trash can. Grand prize for success was an octagonal one.*

Regardless of structure, the best way to make higher-ups aware of your value and to stand out without offending peers is to maximize your contribution. No one can fault you for that.

Contributing starts with committing to your work, mastering the skills your work requires, and, over time, finding your niche. Contributing requires connecting with your manager, colleagues, and industry peers. The strength of your relationships will result in people wanting you to succeed and helping you do so. Finally, contributing requires adding value to your manager, team, and organization: value resulting from achieving your goals, and from "extras" such as showing practical wisdom, bringing in new business, pitching new ideas, and, as you progress, from a deeper understanding of the business. Value such that your presence and contribution *must* be noticed.

If you focus on maximizing your contribution, the more likely you'll be rewarded with greater responsibility and compensation, and the more challenging, impactful, and enjoyable your work will become. Someday you might even earn an octagonal trash can!

> **CONTRIBUTE ROADMAP**
>
> Commit
>
> 1. Engage or Go
> 2. Master Your Job
> 3. Find Your Niche
>
> Connect
>
> 1. Connect with Your Manager
> 2. Connect with Colleagues
> 3. Connect with Industry Peers
>
> Create Value
>
> 1. Perform
> 2. Bring Something Extra
> 3. Master the Business

Commit

Commitment starts with your desire to maximize your contribution and to perform the actions necessary to make that desire a reality. Mere intention—without committing to the actions it will take to make your intention a reality—is easy but ineffective. This combination of intention and action will lead, hopefully, to your finding your niche where you do more of what you do best, and where recognition and rewards follow.

1. Engage or Go

Decide to maximize your contribution. Start with a determination to learn and perform your job. Anything less than your best shortchanges both your employer and you.

From an employer's perspective, employees who "quit and stay" are dead weight. Sooner or later, their lack of commitment is reflected in lack of performance. Competition in business is brutal. Few companies are alone in doing whatever it is they do. Should it appear that money is to be made, others rush in and drive down profits and margins. To survive, let alone thrive, organizations need everyone engaged.

Your objective early in your career is to climb up a steep learning curve. You're in a race to quickly amass skills, ideally transferable ones, that you'll build on for the rest of your working life. Failure to fully engage and develop skills now will be harmful to your potential and earning power later. If you're

not committed to your work, you're wasting irreplaceable time—time you could spend pursuing something more intriguing or exciting that you could willingly commit to.

Assess your commitment. How serious is your commitment, and your promise to yourself to achieve the outcomes you say you want? Worrisome signs include coming in late, taking long lunches, leaving early, spending work time on personal stuff, drooling with your head on the keyboard, and sobbing quietly in the bathroom stall.

> *I knew it was time for me to leave my law firm when I started smoking cigarettes while staring out the window, wishing I was anywhere but at work. I enjoyed my colleagues but couldn't get committed to practicing law.*

More than two-thirds of employees are "Not Engaged" or "Actively Disengaged" at work, according to a Gallup.com poll. Let's hope they don't work at the nuclear power plant or the airport control tower. To assess your commitment, think honestly about your current job satisfaction. Consider:

- Do you dread the start of your work week?
- Does your work interest and challenge you?
- Are you learning skills that you want to learn?
- Can you see yourself doing this work in three years?
- Do you stay current with changes in your field?
- What would it take for you to be more committed?

Put pen to paper to articulate the "why" or "why not" behind your commitment or lack thereof. Your commitment could arise from the work itself. Even if you can't say your work makes a profound difference to the world, are you:

- Doing work and using skills you enjoy?
- Making a difference to clients and customers?
- Working in a physical environment that you like?
- Working with colleagues you learn from and enjoy?

We suspect that if more people did work they enjoy, with people they enjoy, to the benefit of those they interact with, it would make a profound difference to the world.

Your commitment may come not from the work itself, but from an appreciation of the intangibles of your job—autonomy, or flexibility, or the ability to put boundaries on your work, perhaps by being out the door every day at a certain time or by not bringing work home. Or maybe good medical and retirement benefits are important to you and your family, or the opportunity to travel to new and different places. Your commitment may come from the pleasure you take in doing something well.

Don't feel a need to find the work you were "born to do," or get too caught up searching for your "passion." The list of things you can do, and the list of reasons to be excited about whatever you choose, are plentiful. When performed by someone who cares about their work, there's value in most every vocation. And where you are now need not be your forever place. Few of us find such a place, especially early in our careers. It's enough if you're convinced you're in the right place for now.

For me, the magic wasn't in the real estate. It was in working with people I enjoyed and in solving problems, serving customers, and building a profitable company. I suspect we could have been consultants, run a chain of stores, brewed beer, or done most anything else and been excited about our work.

Resolve your commitment. The burden is on you to find what you want to do and where you want to do it, including the organization and the team within it. Commit to what you're doing now. If that's impossible, then leave as soon as practical—thoughtfully and, ideally, without missing a paycheck (see "Advocate").

2. Master Your Job

With the intentional aspect of your commitment resolved, let's focus on the actions required. Start by identifying and acquiring the skills and knowledge necessary to perform your job.

I once heard a sermon entitled "Life's Three Greatest Fears," one of which was "the fear of being found out." I think many of us experience this fear about our work. I know I did when participating in quarterly earnings calls at a publicly held company. More than one hundred analysts would dial in, hear our presentation, and ask probing questions. I feared I would be found wanting. My solution to the fear of being found out? I used my fears as motivators and worked to master my job.

It's a good feeling to be skilled at something and to know it. And so:

Determine the competencies needed for your job. Create a list of the specific skills and knowledge your job requires. These should become apparent as you perform your job, and you may find yourself adding or deleting items as you learn it better. Don't make the list more extensive than necessary because time constraints may prevent you from getting to every item. Prioritize your list, placing the most important items first. Doing this assessment seems simple enough, but most people don't think analytically about the skills and knowledge required for them to succeed.

Devise and execute a personal learning plan. Take responsibility for acquiring the expertise needed to master your job. Don't count on your company to identify the skills and knowledge needed for your position, and then train you. Providing training is expensive, and cost-cutting often reduces formal training. Cutting costs may also saddle bosses with more direct reports, which means less time for employee development. Your manager may assume you were hired because you already possessed the requisite skills and knowledge.

Having made your list of the skills and knowledge required to do your job well, you're now able to identify your gaps and create a plan to close them. As needed, acquire knowledge from various sources. Learn from peers, mentors, and tutors at or outside work, and from optional company training, if provided. Attend seminars and take community college and web-based courses. Read books and trade publications. The demands of your work may mean that you'll be educating yourself on your own time, and dime. But the benefit derived from your supplemental learning will outweigh the cost. It will also help you differentiate yourself from those around you.

Assume that your employer has read and relied on any slight liberties you took with the veracity of your résumé. If your résumé says that you speak fluent Cantonese, you'd best brush up before that conference call with your new client from Hong Kong.

If your job changes or you take on new responsibility, update your list of necessary skills and knowledge and revise your learning plan.

3. Find Your Niche

Young professionals often ask their manager for a roadmap showing the steps in their career progression. There's no harm in asking, "Where have people who started in my position gone next?" Often, however, especially at dynamic, growing places, no such roadmap exists. Don't expect the company to commit to your progression, and don't annoy your manager by repeatedly asking, "What's next for me?" Instead, take responsibility for finding your own path.

Seek a role that requires your best skills. Finding your niche starts with self-knowledge. Pay attention and, over time, identify your natural abilities and strongest skills. Ask yourself, "What are my best skills—the ones upon which I'll build my career?" Determine what you're naturally good at now and what, if nurtured, you might become great at. Almost always this potentially great skill is something you enjoy doing and that comes easier for you than for others. Often it's an ability that others—family members, teachers, coaches, supervisors, peers—have affirmed. Perhaps it is public speaking, or teaching, or leading teams, or being good with numbers and grasping difficult financial concepts. Maybe it's selling. When people tell you how good you are at something, listen to them. If their observations align with your perception of your strengths, look for new and imaginative ways to apply them in your work.

Many organizations offer aptitude testing. Particularly if you haven't done so as an adult, spend a few dollars to have a professional put you through a battery of tests to reveal or confirm your interests and abilities. I went with the non-profit Johnson O'Connor group (and would recommend them). Alternatively, buy a book or find free online tools that help you assess your strengths.

We all have weaknesses that we must shore up as best we can to perform our job. But it's almost impossible to turn weaknesses into strengths. If you're not good with numbers, you may with work become competent, but it's unlikely you'll ever be strong enough to compete with those who are naturally good at numbers, much less differentiate yourself. Instead, you must focus on your strengths, and spend your time and energy building your strengths into your differentiators.

As part of my personal learning plan, I hired an MBA professor at my own expense to tutor me in finance. I improved my finance skills enough to get by, but my boss was a former nuclear submarine officer who could do math in his head about as well as I could on a calculator. So I tried to become exceptional in using skills that came naturally for me and not as much for him.

As you progress, try to move within your organization to a team and a role that is a natural fit, one where the skills required are your best skills, and where you get to do more of what you do best. If this isn't possible, or until it is, try to apply more of what you do best to your current job.

See a need and fill it. When a different role for which you're well suited becomes available, convince others you're the right person for it. Or identify a role that is needed but doesn't yet exist, and sell both the role and your fit for it (see "Pitch" and "Advocate"). Perhaps the role is unappreciated, or represents an opportunity that others don't seem to want. Claim it or create it. "We need it and I'm the one to start it." Then work hard to exceed expectations. You may discover that this area of opportunity requires your best strengths and that you come to love what you do.

Be flexible. To find your niche you may have to move laterally, or even downward for a time. Think of your path not as a corporate ladder that only goes up or down, but as a jungle gym where lots of paths lead to your desired destination. It may be wise to move sideways or serve a stint in another office (even abroad) if doing so allows you to showcase your best skills, broaden your network, develop a deeper understanding of the business, and perhaps even prepare for leadership. Once you've identified your niche, revise your personal learning plan to further develop your natural gifts and skills.

Back in the day more companies had "rotational" programs where new hires spent three to six months in various departments developing a better understanding of the business and perhaps deciding where they might best fit. Such programs are largely gone as businesses decided they were an unnecessary luxury. If you're unhappy in your current role, you may need to pitch a rotation of sorts whereby you move to a different team. I did it at my law firm in an unsuccessful search to find a niche I enjoyed.

Prove what you can do, then consider your next step when opportunities—perhaps of your own creation—become available. Keep showing up, doing your job, learning, and growing. When others see what you can do, the possibilities for your next step may expand. Given natural attrition (people being promoted or self-selecting out), new doors will likely open for you in the next year or two. Your path may lead somewhere more satisfying than you ever could have imagined.

When you love what you do and are grateful for the opportunity to do it, you'll know you've found your niche.

Connect

Relationships are the source of much of our happiness in business and life. Put energy into building them, both internally with your supervisor and with colleagues at all levels, and externally with industry peers.

1. Connect with Your Manager

Your advancement requires the convergence of three things:

1. Opportunity—a position becomes vacant, or a new position is created.
2. Readiness—you're perceived as having the necessary knowledge and skills.
3. Support—someone recommends you, and successfully shepherds your promotion.

In a hierarchical organization, that someone is likely to be your manager. Your talent may be so immense, so undeniable, that you're promoted over the objection of your manager. More likely, your manager gets promoted and recommends you for his role, or acquiesces when a higher-up seeks to move or promote you to another manager's team. For your manager to recommend you for promotion, and to ensure he informs higher-ups of your existence and ability, you must build a positive relationship. Here are some thoughts on how:

Think like your manager. Connection begins by understanding how your manager approaches the many decisions she faces every day. Outsource a function that is now performed by people in-house? Flatten the organization chart by removing levels of management? Promote this person, or that person? Your manager's answer to each question: Do what is best for the company. Her first obligation as a leader is to ensure the survival and success of the mothership. Doing so protects the owners of the company and the livelihood of those who work there and are contributing. Expect her approach to be "company first."

As you interact with your manager, understand this "company first" mindset. When you're a leader—for the good of your team and the company— you'll think the same way when making decisions of every kind.

Work with your manager. Here are thoughts on how to connect when you deal directly with your boss.

Clarify expectations. Consider it your responsibility, not your manager's, to make clear your job responsibilities. Don't make assumptions about your goals, deadlines, what your work product is expected to look like, where you are to be and by when, or anything else important to your role. Seek to understand the criteria upon which your performance will be evaluated. Clarify expectations so you can meet them and avoid unpleasant surprises.

> *As a young lawyer, I was providing litigation support on a defective tire case. The client didn't want the expense of paying me to sit in court during the three-week trial, so I remained back at the office. Although no one told me, I was expected to make myself available every day when the court broke for lunch. One day my presence was demanded when I was out of the office enjoying Taco Tuesday. A serious butt-kicking followed.*

If your manager doesn't make clear your goals, then create a goals document and call for a discussion. Even if you must write it, your objective is to have a document that the two of you agree will serve as the basis of your performance review.

Stay in communication. If you're your own boss, or work closely with your boss every day, staying in communication isn't an issue. If you work for a larger organization where contact with your boss is less frequent, stay in communication throughout the year. You want to be visible, so do not hide. Some

managers establish standing meetings with their reports. If yours doesn't, then call for progress meetings. How often you do so will be influenced by your manager's willingness to meet with you. Perhaps, at first, if given the opportunity, meet too often versus too little. Eventually the two of you will find a comfortable rhythm.

For each progress meeting, create and follow a one-page agenda. Email the agenda in advance and bring a copy for your manager. Expect your manager to have a list of items she wants to discuss. You're not likely to see these in advance. Complete your manager's list first to ensure you know what's on her mind. When you get to your list, inform your manager of your progress and challenges. Keep your portion of the meetings brief.

What if your manager declines your overtures to meet on a regular basis? Some managers dislike the "people" aspects of their job and avoid meetings. If so, develop a standard format and write an update as needed. If you're involved in a critical, time-sensitive project, "as needed" could be as frequent as a daily email. If you're working steadily toward the realization of annual goals, your updates could be monthly. Communicate with whatever frequency is needed to keep your manager informed and to receive timely input.

Provide candid input. When your manager says, "What do you think?" or "I'd like your input," recognize the opportunity and engage. You want to become someone whose thoughts are solicited on matters of consequence. Give candid input in a respectful, organized manner. If you're unsure whether your manager knows the facts, start there. Knowledge of and agreement on the facts is necessary for sound decisions and effective action. Give the facts first and then, with context established, offer your opinion. When your input isn't requested, interject if needed to prevent "grievous error" (lawyer term for a major screw-up).

Take responsibility. Your boss wants performance, not excuses. Don't blame others when something that was your responsibility goes awry. Your boss doesn't want to hear, "It's my responsibility, but Joe in Accounting said he was going to handle that."

This kind of ass-covering doesn't work much better: "It wasn't my fault." "I emailed you about that." "That's not how we've done it before." "That'll never work." "I guess I wasn't thinking."

Disclose. Disclosure is your friend, even when it's embarrassing. Ask for help when you need it. It's OK from time to time to say, "I don't know," "I don't understand," or "I need help." And, "Please show me, one time." If you're in over your head, and you think your manager needs or would want to know you're struggling, speak up. It beats floundering and failing.

If you see something that concerns you, speak up. Especially if you're the cause of a powder-keg situation. Don't try to defuse it on your own before it explodes. Your manager can't provide wisdom and resources to solve undisclosed problems, and your delay in disclosing may waste precious time that makes addressing the situation more difficult. Good leaders insist on knowing bad news in a timely fashion and look unfavorably upon those who knew but failed to say something.

Bring problems with a recommended solution. When you bring problems to your manager, don't just drop a steaming cow pie and depart. The CEO of a major construction company was fired on the spot when he told his board, "We've got a huge problem here, and I have no idea what to do." You'll get more slack at your level, but always come with options and a plan. Even if your manager doesn't accept your plan, you'll have given the problem thought—and sharing your options could start a brainstorming session with your manager that results in a better plan.

Be the detail person. To successfully achieve a goal or complete a project, someone must get into the weeds, master the details, and take care of things others didn't think of. Likely that will not be your manager; it will be you. Being the detail person doesn't mean giving long-winded explanations of what you've done, hoping for credit or praise. It means seeing and doing what needs to be done.

Respect your manager's time. Don't ask for your manager's time unless needed, and don't take more time than you asked for. Stick to business, get to the point, and keep it moving in conversations, voicemails, and emails. Try to answer questions with a yes or no, and then explain. Be mindful of which meetings you ask your boss to attend and do your best to ensure they're productive.

At my request, my boss drove ninety minutes to meet with a potential buyer of one of our apartment communities. After hearing the offer, my boss replied that the buyer must have been under the mistaken impression that we would entertain a distressed sales price. We would not. The meeting lasted maybe five minutes, thanks mostly to pleasantries on the front end. It was a quiet drive back.

Support your manager. Connection with your manager also requires that you help her succeed. Supporting your manager is part of what your organization is paying you to do and what you'll expect from your team when you're a leader.

Be positive. Every team needs a spark. If you're dynamic and gifted with a sense of humor, use your infectious style to add life to conversations, meetings, and projects. You can be equally supportive if you're more introverted, and your forte is thinking quietly, deeply, and tenaciously about problems until you solve them. Whatever your personality, bring a can-do, we'll-figure-it-out attitude. Likely your boss would much prefer an enthusiastic optimist to a grim realist who has all the answers why something can't be done. Let a positive attitude be part of who you are and what you bring.

Because of your relatively young age, more optimism and enthusiasm will be expected from you than from the middle-aged guy three cubicles down who is negotiating his third divorce settlement, with overdue credit card bills and a kid in rehab.

Take initiative. The more ways you contribute, the better. Your job description—if there was one—went into a drawer and became irrelevant the day you started. You'll likely be asked to do things you didn't expect. Perhaps you'll be asked to take trips, give presentations, meet with clients, fire a vendor, research a new business idea, or even move temporarily to a different city to help establish a new office. To the extent you can accommodate such requests, and cheerfully so, you'll engender good will. So, too, if you see something that needs to be done and you can do it, do so. Likely you'll do things your manager may not know about or appreciate. Here's betting he knows more than you think.

Contribute in meetings. Start by doing the advance reading and being prepared. If you haven't done the reading, it will be risky for you to express a viewpoint. Sitting there, contributing nothing, hoping not to be exposed is a terrible feeling.

Those inclined to be bolder—and not cower in silence—may wish to borrow a strategy I perfected during my first year of law school. If unprepared for the day, I would volunteer my thoughts early in class, perhaps by answering an easy question or by piggybacking on a classmate's answer. ("You know, Professor, I agree with Susie's comment.") In theory, my professor would register my participation as proof that I was prepared, and then move on to other students. This technique is not without risk— one equally applicable to your business meeting.

Next, be on time. A no-nonsense meeting host will start the meeting precisely when scheduled out of respect for those who showed up on time and to make a point. Now, be fully present. Whether the meeting is in person, by teleconference, or by video conference, put away your phone. Assert yourself when you have something relevant or insightful to say; otherwise, listen. Don't speak just to draw attention to yourself, but do recognize that if you rarely contribute it will be noticed. Higher-ups will wonder why you were invited and whether you don't have something better to do (like make them money).

If a meeting gets bogged down in the past, move it to the future tense (see "Pitch"). "What are we going to do?" is usually the operative question, more so than "Who's at fault?" or "How did we get here?" Don't monopolize the conversation; don't lead the group down rabbit holes; and don't engage in private conversations that distract and annoy your manager (or meeting sponsor). The prize for being a significant meeting contributor is that you may get invited to more meetings. That's a good thing, as one day you'll be leading them (see "Lead"). To prepare for that day, observe and make notes on what those running the meetings do that works and doesn't work.

Complement your manager's skills. It's unlikely that you and your manager have identical skill sets. Look for something he needs, and may not excel at, where you can increase your contribution. Perhaps you can complement your boss with stronger technology, analytical, or writing skills. You're on the right track to providing complementary skills when your manager says to you, "And that's why we're a great team."

Reflect well on your manager. In sports a player's talent is sometimes overshadowed by off-the-field conduct that embarrasses the coach and the organization. Your manager is entitled to set standards as to how business is to be conducted on her team. Learn and reflect what your boss expects by observing how she thinks, writes, speaks, and deals with people. Speak well about your manager to others.

Don't let your boss make errors you can prevent. When gospel and soul singer Mavis Staples performed at UNC Chapel Hill, she twice told the crowd how wonderful it was to be in Raleigh. Raleigh is twenty-five miles away and home to rival NC State. When she started for a third time to mention Raleigh, a back-up vocalist whispered in her ear, and must have said, "Mavis, we're in Chapel Hill." She smiled and gracefully recovered. The back-up singer protected his boss.

Rise to the occasion during trying times. There will be times when your company is under duress and the business world, and perhaps the press, are watching. Such times might follow a natural disaster, network attack, or product tampering that puts at risk the safety of your customers or employees, or their property, or private data. Or maybe your company is merging, going public, or fighting an unwelcome takeover bid.

See these moments as an opportunity. Ask your manager what you can do to help or, if he's not available, just find a way to pitch in and help your colleagues successfully navigate the situation. Be fully present when all hands are needed most. Hopefully your recognition of the importance of the moment, and your response, will be remembered and later rewarded. More certain is that those who were unresponsive will be unfavorably remembered.

Now that you've connected with your manager, let's do the same with those you work with.

2. Connect with Colleagues

You need the support of your co-workers—including peers—to be effective in your job and to advance. Their opinion of you may be solicited, and if they view you with apathy or hostility your advancement may be jeopardized. Perhaps you've heard the expression "No one would piss on him if he was on fire." Make sure that your colleagues would extinguish the flames, and even be quick about it. To make your team stronger and higher-functioning because of your presence, fit in while standing out.

Fit in. Getting along with people is an essential soft skill. It allows you to be more effective, build bridges between people, and make your workplace a more enjoyable place.

Be appropriate in manners, speech, and dress. Good manners and well-chosen words are always appropriate and never go out of style. Discern when formality is required and when informality is permitted. If in doubt, go with formality. Be thoughtful with your word choice, and, no matter the workplace custom, go easy on the expletives. As to dress, your clothes don't need to make a statement—they simply need to be appropriate.

> *I've seen "Business Casual" and "Jeans Friday" (or jeans everyday) lead many astray. Some guys pair baggy mom jeans with a plaid flannel shirt and look like Larry the Lumberjack; others—both men and women—create a sharp look in jeans, starting with great shoes (your mom was right about the importance of shoes). Even if allowed, shorts and hairy legs aren't a great look. Neither is cleavage. There's no harm in always dressing a little better than required.*

Cultivate a presence that suggests you're destined for greater things and will represent the company well if suddenly asked to meet with a key client or board member. Take advantage of modern dentistry, use mouthwash and deodorant, leave the fuzzy slippers at home, flush the office toilet after using, and don't steal people's food from the breakroom fridge. If the founder is a conservative Baptist, remember, no dancing.

Be a decent human being. People who have a choice avoid those who are rude, difficult, or unreasonable to be with nicer, more congenial people. So be friendly, flexible, and generous. Be grateful, and thank people who help you. Be humble—let others extol your virtues and your accomplishments. Should you provoke unsolicited criticism from a colleague, be curious, not furious. Ask yourself if there's some truth to what was said, or implied, and, if so, learn from it. Cultivate self-awareness, social awareness, and self-management.

Genuine interest in other people goes a long way toward building rapport, so listen more than you talk. Those who listen effectively handle situations differently, and with better results, than those who don't. They learn more and—sometimes helpful—reveal less. Develop an awareness of when you've talked enough, especially about yourself. Flip a one-sided conversation to let the other person talk. Asking good questions is an effective way to listen and learn.

Apologize when necessary. No one likes a know-it-all who can never be wrong or admit a mistake. Stop if you find yourself saying, "All I said was." You're sounding defensive, and likely you've offended. If an apology is required to restore good feelings, do so quickly, graciously, and completely. The words aren't hard—"I was wrong to . . . I am sorry. Please forgive me." A proper apology doesn't contain the word "but" or blame the other person for taking what you said the "wrong way."

Do favors and return favors. Give value for value when trading favors with colleagues and industry peers, and do things for people who can't repay you. The most appreciated favor is often the one you do for another's son or daughter.

Promote collegiality. Try to build a positive relationship with everyone. Treat everyone with respect, starting with the security and cleaning crews at your building. Treat all colleagues as partners, including the receptionist and administrative assistants. Spend time with colleagues and get to know them. Use your contact software to makes notes about people you meet—their family members, interests, activities, memberships, friends. Use this information to build relationships more quickly. A peer or someone who is below you now, or someone who reports to you when you become a manager, may one day be your manager.

Speak well of team members to others during conversations whether they're present or absent. Give colleagues the benefit of the doubt and assume good intent. When a question arises about a colleague's conduct, withhold judgment until you know the facts. Compliment co-workers on work well done, and connect people by passing on the compliments of others.

Help teammates when asked, and when you see a need. Those new to the company or the industry will likely welcome and benefit from your insight and encouragement. When others help you, show genuine appreciation and look for opportunities to reciprocate.

> *When I transitioned from law to real estate, a peer took me and another newbie aside and gave us a real estate finance tutorial of his own creation. He didn't have to do this and gained nothing tangible from doing it. I still remember this kindness. How can you help a colleague?*

Work to see both sides. Perhaps the primary benefit of a legal education is developing the ability to see the other person's point of view. Spare yourself the pain and debt of law school and develop this skill on the job. Be in tune with how your colleagues think, what they believe, and why they believe it.

Disagree agreeably. To contribute, you must say what you think, which sometimes means disagreeing (even when you see both sides). It's hard to contribute and differentiate if all you do is constantly affirm what others say. Disagree in a civil tone and keep it business, not personal.

Stand out. Doing great work is essential to earning the respect of your superiors. It's also a building block for standing out. But doing great work by itself is unlikely to set you apart. To distinguish themselves in some other way, people seek to be, or to be seen as being:

- Smarter—by displaying superior mental firepower that is apparent to all;
- More dedicated—by arriving early, staying late, working nights and weekends;
- More connected—by ceaselessly networking and creating a larger network.

Being smart, however, is out of your control, and smarts alone ensure nothing. You do need to be dedicated and diligent, which sometimes the super-smart fail to grasp. And you do need to connect and network. But being smart (enough), dedicated, and connected are expected, and are not reliable sources of differentiation.

Instead, differentiate through character. In any company, some people are trusted more than others. Earn the trust—and respect—of your manager and colleagues by acting with integrity in all matters and at all times. The ancients called it "*ethos*," meaning argument by character.

When we hired, especially for higher positions, we looked first for character. Usually multiple candidates had the requisite skills and, if not, we could teach skills. We couldn't teach character, and so we sought people who would do the right thing when no one was watching, and who would reflect our values when dealing with those inside and outside the company.

Aristotle said the way to develop character is through "*habituation*"— repeating virtuous acts until you do them without thinking. He believed one becomes honest by behaving honestly, unselfish by doing unselfish things, and self-disciplined by performing acts of personal discipline. To differentiate through character, develop these habits:

Have principles and adhere to them. Begin by asking, "What do I stand for? What will I refuse to tolerate? When will I speak up?" It's easier, of course, to adhere to principles when times are good and your principles aren't challenged. It's not so easy when you're instructed to do something you know is wrong, when taking a stand puts you at risk, or when, under pressure, you're tempted to do something unethical. During stressful times recognize when your principles are under attack so that you can thoughtfully respond.

Be honest in all matters, large and small. This doesn't mean being "honest" in the sense of saying all you think and being rude. It means being truthful and not misleading others by acts of commission or omission. Don't say you

did something when you didn't (or vice versa). Don't profess to have knowledge or skills that you don't. Don't say you know people when you don't. If you prove dishonest in small matters, your boss and teammates will be wary about trusting you with larger ones.

Judges face disciplinary action under their Model Code of Judicial Conduct for creating the "appearance of impropriety." It's a good test for the rest of us. If you must explain why your conduct that appears dubious isn't dubious, skip the conduct. Your explanation is likely futile, as the need to explain suggests impropriety.

Do what you say you will do. Don't commit to do something unless you will perform. Be mindful to keep your word when you promise to do something, send something, be somewhere, make or return a call, or meet a deadline. If in doubt about your intention or ability, don't promise. Breaking even a small promise may negatively influence a relationship in a lasting way.

Renegotiate deadlines, if you must, in advance. If you're going to miss a deadline—defined as anything large or small you committed to do by a certain time—tell the affected person before the time arrives and try to negotiate a new deadline. In the absence of advance disclosure, the logical assumption is you'll meet your deadline.

Spend company money as you would your own. If you wouldn't spend your own money sitting in a certain class of airline seat, or staying at a certain hotel, or going to a certain restaurant, or ordering a certain bottle of wine, don't do it on your company's dime. Frugality, both personal and corporate, is a good habit. Once you become a leader, insist that your team apply the same test to their spending.

If you're 6'4" flying to Amsterdam for a conference, it's reasonable to ask for Comfort Class to get an extra four inches of precious legroom. Doing so passes the test—if you would spend your money when flying there on vacation.

Don't commit in advance to respect a confidence. If you're asked to promise "not to tell anyone" before hearing a secret, the short answer is, "that depends." Your job—or a legal or ethical obligation—may require you to do something

about what you're told. A better answer is: "I will respect your confidence unless I feel I have a duty to do something about it." If you promise to respect a confidence after hearing it, keep your word.

So, too, beware asking other people to hold something "in confidence." If you find yourself doing this, ask why? Why are you exposing yourself to the risk that they won't respect your confidence? What benefit outweighs this very real risk? Are you asking that something be held in confidence because you're about to violate a confidence you were entrusted with?

Demonstrate strength of character until it's part of who you are and how you're known. Be vigilant because, once tarnished, perception of character is hard to restore. Some are cavalier, saying, "That's just who I am—you get the gristle with the gravy." Folks who make such an argument don't want to address their character shortcomings. Working with people daily means the real you will be discovered. Make it worth discovering.

While fitting in likely feels comfortable, don't be reluctant to stand out. Advancement usually isn't a zero-sum game vis-à-vis your colleagues. If you're promoted, your teammates aren't demoted; presumably they carry on until they too are promoted, or a job opens in another department, or they choose to leave to join another company. While you may on occasion compete with someone for the same position, you and your rival have different skills, career aspirations, and priorities. Usually there's a good place for all who contribute. Stay positive until you're promoted; do your best, see what happens, and then reassess your commitment.

3. Connect with Industry Peers

Make friends throughout your industry. Your success depends on who you are, what you can do, and who you know. Today's industry peer could be your co-worker or boss tomorrow. Some of your contemporaries will be running companies in the future. You'll be doing business with them, and you may want to hire or be hired by them. And you'll want to borrow ideas from them. So make friends with peers who work for competitors and vendors, particularly with people who do what you do at leading companies. Often the primary benefit of attending industry conferences isn't listening to the speakers. It's meeting new people and attending meetings you set up in advance or during the conference.

Create a favorable first impression. The way you greet people affects their impression of you. As you make friends out there, look people in the eye and shake their hand. Unless you're sure a person knows your name, help her by opening with your name.

If you find yourself at one of those dreadful cocktail "networking" events, challenge yourself to identify and talk to a few people you want to meet. All you need is a handshake and a hello to allow for follow-up. You likely don't need a business card to find their contact info online. While connecting with industry peers is easier if your work allows you to attend industry events (more likely as you advance), start now to build relationships outside your organization.

Put people together. Introduce and connect industry friends by acting as a "middleperson." Bring people together to their mutual benefit, even though you gain no benefit. Both parties will remember the favor.

Find the right networking tool. As we write, LinkedIn seems to be the gold standard of technology tools for networking. Whichever networking tools you use:

- Ensure your profile is professional and current, and your picture is flattering.
- Seek out opportunities to meet people in person.
- Prior to meeting new people, review their online profile to look for mutual friends, things you have in common, and unusual skills or interests.
- If in your reading you find an article the person might find interesting, bring it as a gift; if you learn of an interest when you meet, send such an article afterwards.
- If there is something you can readily do to help your new contact, do so.
- After meeting new people, send a follow-up email or invite them to connect online.
- Be mindful not to share proprietary information, even when your two companies don't directly compete.

Networking is an accelerant in building relationships and will be essential when you move into leadership. Should you choose to do so, modern technology makes it easy to connect with industry peers.

Create Value

1. Perform

When the John Deere Company was criticized for eliminating franchisees, some of which were family businesses that had been with Deere for generations, then-CEO Robert Lane responded: "For years we talked about Deere as a family. The fact is, we are not a family. What we are is a high-performance

team . . . If someone is not pulling their weight, you're not on the high-performance team anymore." Intentions don't matter. Commitment and connection must translate into action and results.

Work hard. Dwayne Johnson (aka "the Rock") says: "I'm always asked, 'What's the secret to success?' But there are no secrets. Be humble. Be hungry. And always be the hardest worker in the room." The Rock's wisdom is confirmed by a study of millionaires who identified "Hard work, more than most people" as one of their five "most important" success factors.

These same millionaires identified as "least important" to their success attending a top-rated college, having a superior IQ, or being lucky. Their average GPA was a 2.9 (on a 4.0 scale) with an SAT score of 1190 (on a 1600 scale).

Successful people are more likely to drive to and from work in the dark rather than show up at nine and rush out the door at five. Assume that hard work is expected and required to perform your job well. We often can't control the achievement of the outcomes we seek. We always can control the effort and attitude we bring to any opportunity or problem.

A few years back UNC head basketball coach Roy Williams, unhappy with his team's lethargic play, remarked that he was having to coach effort, and that he wasn't accustomed to this kind of coaching. Your manager may be unwilling to coach effort. Effort is expected.

Do work when you're at work. Web-surfing, tweeting, online shopping, gaming, filling out your NCAA March Madness tournament bracket, tweaking your fantasy football lineup, keeping up with "breaking news," and all the other intriguing things you can do online consume time and diminish your output. Don't forget that every site you visit is being recorded somewhere, including the ones where you're posting your résumé.

Work smart. The number of hours you work is meaningful only to the extent that you use them effectively. Spend your time on the tasks that create the most value and move you fastest to achieving your goals. Work on what's difficult, creative, and impactful, including your personal learning plan. Cut the non-essentials from your to-do list. And take the time (and suffer the aggravation and initial time-suck) to master productivity tools that allow you to work smarter and save time in the long run.

Deliver work you're proud to put your name on. Whatever you take on, including mundane work and work you volunteer for, do it well. You can't build a career on "usually" doing excellent work. Exceed expectations. Do more than asked—do what is needed to achieve the desired objective instead of turning out lackluster work to put a "check in the box." Even if you're tired, unmotivated, or overcommitted, see your deliverables through to conclusion. Proof documents, double-check numbers, perfect slides, and practice presentations. Try to do it right the first time to save yourself the time and embarrassment of doing it over.

Don't be fooled by a boss with a sense of humor into thinking that her standards aren't high, or that much isn't expected of you. Remember the professor who was entertaining, but whose exam crushed you? Don't let your guard down.

Get results. Don't confuse activity with productivity. Absent results, most organizations will not continue to fund you.

As my first boss in real estate explained, "I don't care whether you're lucky or good, or even whether you work hard. I suggest you work hard, but what matters is that you achieve your goals. Otherwise, I can't afford you." A business friend was told by his mentor, "You're on a path to get let go. I know you're working hard, but you're not getting results."

The unpleasant reality is that we're all paid to produce!

Stay focused. Don't coast after success. Your company continues to pay you and expects performance in return. If you ease up after a win, thinking you've earned the right, you're risking the reputation you worked so hard to build. Business is a "What have you done for me lately?" proposition.

Learn from mistakes. Failure is instructive, perhaps even more so when it's embarrassing. Sometimes failure allows you to change course and prevent a greater failure later. If you learn from your mistakes so that you don't repeat them, odds are good your job won't be in jeopardy. Your company has made an investment in you, and your contribution likely outweighs by a wide margin the cost of your mistakes. But as the expression goes, "Even a mule walks around the hole the second time."

Like you, I've never heard this expression before.

2. Bring Something Extra

Bring something to your work that helps set you apart and gets you noticed, such as:

Show practical wisdom. While minding your own character, look for clues that provide insight into the character of those you deal with. If you miss them, your naïveté may cost you.

If it seems too good to be true, assume it's false until proven otherwise. Whether it's a promised sales price, service level standard, employment offer, return on investment, or inducement of any kind, beware of promises that deviate materially from historical norms or from whatever is currently "market." Otherwise, you'll likely be disappointed, if not deceived.

My neighbor Jack received a phishing call telling him he'd won a new Cadillac. After showing great elation, and before the caller could explain what he had to do to get it, my friend asked what color it was. The caller, after floundering a bit, asked my friend why he wanted to know. The reply: "Because I won a blue Cadillac last week, and I don't want two the same color."

Consider incentives. What are the motives of the person asking you to part with your money, time, or resources to buy, sell, lease, join, or invest? Is he disinterested? If not, whose interest is primary? If your interests aren't aligned, be skeptical of the bargain offered.

Beware of easy explanations and glib generalizations. The answer to any complex question begins with "That depends" followed by questions that allow the one asked to provide a more thoughtful answer. Generalizations without supporting facts and details may reveal sloppy thinking or a lack of understanding. In contracts, fuzzy language may suggest a desire to avoid enforceable obligations.

Look for proof of experience and results. Find out if the person has successfully done for others, or for herself, what she proposes to do for you. Be wary of promises of those who can't demonstrate that they have both the experience and track record to warrant your business.

Send liars packing. If someone lies to you, consider their motive. Is there some exculpatory explanation? If you discern a pattern of lies, their character is now revealed, and you're on notice not to trust them. Do whatever you can to remove them from your business and your life. Hopefully, it's not your boss!

> *Beware too of those who make a public show of their faith. They may believe they're devout, and maybe they are, but trusting them in business matters because they profess to be religious is unwise. They may be trying to use their faith to get something from you that your judgment would otherwise reject.*

Bring in new business. New business seldom arrives miraculously at your door. Somebody ventured into the world and made it rain. The sooner you help bring business to your company, the more valuable and recession-resistant you become. You're never too new in your job to start bringing in business for your organization. The law of attraction holds that if you're looking for new business in your networking—unlike peers who aren't—you're likely to find it.

> *Most young attorneys give little thought to where the files on their desk come from. They show up expecting work to do without appreciating that someone made those files happen. They don't realize that they, too, are expected to generate business for the firm.*

Do something special. Generate and pitch new ideas (see "Pitch"), source great people for the company, or volunteer for challenging projects or assignments. And, every now and then, undertake and succeed at something difficult that adds great value.

> *When a young development associate, I was able to save a project by first amending the Raleigh City Code to allow a density transfer and then buying density units from an adjacent landowner. It was an unexpected outcome that transformed a loss of millions of dollars into a profit. This "something special" didn't save my job when the next recession rolled around, but it led my boss's boss to find another home for me in the company.*

3. Master the Business

Seek a deeper understanding. Automotive innovator Carl Sewell observes, "The reason most people fail in business is because they do not really understand their business." McDonald's founder Ray Kroc said his business was real estate, not hamburgers. Rolex CEO Andre Heiniger said he was in the luxury business, not the watch business. What business are you in? Who are your customers—the buyers of your product or service, a middleperson, shareholders, or someone else? It's hard to deliver great customer service without prioritizing your customers and considering their respective needs.

If you like the line of work you've chosen, seek to understand it at a deeper level. Go beyond mastering your job to mastering your business. Learn what factors drive the business. Learn its vocabulary and understand its key metrics. Learn its history. Think about where your industry is headed, what challenges and opportunities lie ahead, and what your company must do to remain relevant. Ready yourself now for success later when you take on a greater role.

A developer friend tells a story about walking through a competitor's under-construction apartment community at 6:00 am. He wanted to see the units and understand the latest generation of his competitor's product. Startled by a sound behind him, he turned to see an industry peer doing the same thing. This is what mastering your business looks like. It's not in a job description. It's seeking a deeper understanding to excel in your chosen line of work.

Your manager may push you to become competent in your job, but likely no one will push you to master your business and envision its future. Differentiating yourself from others in these ways is up to you.

Conclusion

It's been brought to my attention that Cosmopolitan *magazine offers "love tests" to see whether someone is a worthy partner, and whether the relationship measures up: "Do you take risks in love?" "Are you in love or forcing it?" "What is his intimacy IQ?" (Uh-oh, trouble brewing here.) Maybe the ultimate love test is never asking your partner to take a love test.*

Business has its own love tests. Would your colleagues miss you if you were gone? Would your manager:

1. Say you're worth what you're paid?
2. Care if you left to work for the competition?
3. Invite you to join if starting her own company?

Not easy tests, with each more difficult than the last. How do you fare?

Here's an even tougher test. After a speech, Mr. Trammell Crow was asked, "What do you look for in a business partner?" His business model involved selecting partners in major cities and funding them to create a local real estate business. The audience expected him to say he looked for someone with a track record of success, with local knowledge and contacts, or with access to capital. Mr. Crow's answer: "Someone who I would be comfortable with raising my children in my absence." A profound reply. Isn't that the kind of person each of us wants to work with and to be?

The journey to develop your skills, and to master both your job and your business, is a challenging and ongoing process. As you gain skills and knowledge, you'll increase your contribution to your manager, your team, and your company. You'll also lower your stress level, enjoy your work more, and eventually, find your niche and do more of what you do best.

Application: The Horrible Boss

We all want bosses who are conscientious, hard-working, and fair, and who care about their people. Yet there are plenty of bosses out there who make people's lives miserable and whose ascension defies logic. Such bosses from hell make it difficult to contribute, but there are ways to survive them.

Perhaps you've encountered the:

- Backstabber, who marginalizes team members by downplaying their accomplishments or claiming them as his own;
- Belittler, who dresses people down in front of peers and criticizes even when praising;
- Manipulator, who manages up beautifully to her boss but is a tyrant to her team;
- Narcissist, who brings an oversized ego, a need for admiration, and a lack of empathy;
- Screamer, who is volatile and unpredictable, and for whom no work is good enough;
- Workaholic, who works insane hours and expects his people to do likewise.

Or the weird, the paranoid, or the dishonest. Or some toxic combination of the above. Good bosses have much in common; bad bosses are bad in their own way. One thing bad bosses have in common is their demoralizing effect on their people. So what can you do?

Maintain perspective. No boss is perfect, but is yours so bad that you must leave? Is he abusive or dishonest, or someone you don't trust to be fair? Or is he just not the boss you had hoped for? When you get a discouraging review, or fail to get a promotion you think you deserve, or when a restructuring changes what you are doing, be more thoughtful than emotional. Assess your new prospects. Don't lose sight of what's good about the job you still have.

Consider your options.

Ride it out, for now. You like your job and the company—it's your boss you can't stand. Perhaps you see some bigger picture that warrants riding it out. If so, be resilient. Stay, waiting until your manager moves to a new role, or you do. Continue to contribute. This, too, you hope, shall pass.

Try harder to make the relationship work. Consider meeting with your manager to discuss ways the two of you can work together more effectively (see "Advocate"). Given your situation, consider how candid you want to be, the

likely outcomes from such a discussion, and the best timing if you decide to proceed.

Transfer to another department. At the first opportunity, move to someone else's purview even if it means transferring sideways, or even down. Start looking now for a landing spot and get yourself ready by creating and working your learning plan. Before initiating a transfer, find out all you can about your prospective boss. Then judge whether her management style will fit well with your personality.

Expose your manager's lack of suitability. This is a nuclear option best exercised as a last resort after much thought and soul-searching. Hence the saying, "If you come at the king, you best not miss." Do you think that those up the ladder will side with you over your manager? Unless there has been serious, demonstrable malfeasance, not likely. More likely, you'll soon be looking for a new job. If you have a mentor or sounding board you trust, this is a good time to seek guidance.

Leave for another job or to get more education. Seek a job that uses more of your best skills and gets you closer to finding your niche. And perhaps that pays more. Be mindful of the economic cycle when timing your departure, as recessions come around more often than you might think. If you're leaving to start your own thing and you believe you have the resources, financial stability, and skills to do so, then go for it. Otherwise, absent fraud or other conduct you can't be part of, don't quit your job before you get another one. You don't know how long the downtime between jobs will be and, if a recession hits while you're job hunting, you could be out of work for years. Consider also:

- Do I need a paycheck?
- Am I learning new skills or gaining valuable knowledge?
- Am I connecting with new people who might open new doors?

You may not want a gap in income, learning, or networking. If you're convinced you cannot do your present job while looking for a new one, see if you can work part-time for your company while pursuing your job search.

Our condolences if you're in such an intolerable situation that your best option is to leave (for how to do so, see "Advocate"). Given the increased frequency with which young professionals are changing jobs, our ability to obtain references, market ourselves, and navigate the hiring process will need to be among our many competencies.

Question and Answer

1. What about office politics?

Is seeking to maximize one's contribution insufficient or naïve? Must one play politics? Hopefully not, but maybe—just a little.

Learn the system where you work. As part of its culture, every organization has its own buzzwords and jargon, as well as a system to know, work within, and maneuver around. Who must approve or support something, regardless of what the organization chart says? What will and won't the company spend money on? Which department consistently produces the senior leaders of tomorrow? What is and isn't valued in an employee? Is integrity demanded, or is cutting corners condoned or even expected? To advance past a certain point, must one have an MBA, law, or other degree or certification? Is the company committed to a diverse workforce?

Figure out what is valued at your organization and do it. Most companies have behaviors that are expected, and that lead to personal success. Pay attention and learn what they are where you work.

Look for role models. Observe those who are rising stars—What are they doing to get ahead? What can you learn from them? What behaviors could you start or stop now to contribute more?

Expect rationality to ultimately prevail. The presence of some system does not alter the reality that your success—at your current place of employment, your next place of employment, or your own company—depends on maximizing your contribution. Meritocracy may be "out of whack" for a time, or at any given time, but ultimately exceptional performers will be recognized. So, too, non-performers will be identified and dismissed, no matter what their ploys to stay employed. Survival of the company and the jobs, income, and perks of those at the top depend upon advancing the best and letting the mediocre go. For you, rationality means that people will eventually realize what an asset you've become. If that doesn't happen, consider going someplace where people appreciate your value.

2. I've been offered a promotion! Now what?

Well done and congrats! But first:

Think carefully before taking a position with high turnover. As best you can, determine the story behind such short tenures. Can anyone, for example, coach the sorry Detroit Lions to a conference championship? Taking that job

has proven to be career suicide. As you consider your new position, you may find opportunity or, sadly, discover unrealistic expectations, lack of company support, or some other reason that likely dooms the seat-holder to failure. Likewise, think carefully before taking a position with a team that has little room for improvement. If the team is already high-performing, there may be little opportunity for you to differentiate.

Assuming that your vetting dispels any anxieties, and that you accept the promotion:

Don't do your old job. It may be comfortable initially to keep doing what you've already demonstrated you're good at, and that led to your promotion, but your focus now needs to be on the challenges of this new job. As before, figure out the competencies required to succeed and create a personal learning plan.

Connect with your new boss in ways that earn you credibility. Your good reputation may precede you, but your new boss will form her own opinion as she assesses your work and how you interact with others. Recognize and accept that your work world has changed. In a sense you're starting over; commit yourself to establishing a good connection.

Be worth the premium as you become more expensive over time. Being paid more is a good thing, but over time the gap between your compensation and that of a less expensive employee will widen. Continue to find new ways to contribute to help ensure someone doesn't focus on you when looking to lower costs.

Be wary of making continued advancement a prerequisite for continued commitment. Pyramids narrow at the top. We can't all run the show. Someone else may get the spot you seek, or someone whom dynamite couldn't dislodge may be in that spot. You may need to find growth within your current job and, eventually, change your job in ways that maintain your interest and motivate you to contribute more.

3. What about work-life balance?

Balancing work and life outside work is about priorities. You've got lots of priorities in your life. There's work, but there's also family, friends, and fun. And, perhaps, faith, community, travel, and more. There are trade-offs between compensation, lifestyle, and job satisfaction. It's tough to make a boatload of money, go home at 5:00 pm, and work for Teach for America, all at the same time. High-paying jobs often come with long hours and, for some, less personal satisfaction. What you value most and how you allocate your

limited resource of time is a deeply personal decision. Some people can't wait to go home at the end of the work day; others find it more rewarding to be at work rather than at home. How you wish to allocate your time will likely ebb and flow as people, circumstances, and priorities in your life change.

Some companies will fit your priorities and desired lifestyle; others won't. Some will be more enlightened, and flexible about scheduling, than others. Some will provide more in-office or on-campus resources than others, making the workplace environment friendlier and more supportive. Even the most supportive of employers—those who are more nurturing, who encourage you to have a life outside the office, and who understand and support you in times of personal crisis—expect you to do your work at a high level absent such an occasional crisis. There's a business to be run, one that affects the economic fortunes of many stakeholders, and your contribution is expected.

So don't expect your employer to be too concerned with—much less resolve—your desired balance of priorities. Just as you're responsible for managing your career, so, too, you're responsible for balancing your priorities.

For young professionals today, the line between "work life" and "personal life" is blurry, and chasing some ratio of work-life balance is an elusive if not impossible pursuit. Sometimes your professional life will require more of your time, and other times it may be less demanding. It's a wonderful feeling when we're able to integrate work and personal life such that they complement each other and aren't in competition, and we're happy with both.

4. Any final tips and tricks?

Be known for something positive that matters. Perhaps it's giving effective presentations, getting deals closed, finding capital, soothing anxious clients or investors, mentoring new associates, or giving insightful feedback on company communications. Something where you're known as the go-to person.

Get over the fear of looking stupid. Ask questions to your manager, peers, mentors, or anyone else about things you want to learn. A study shows that many people don't ask for help or advice to avoid looking incompetent, even though they realize doing so would increase their chances of success. The study further shows, ironically, that people who ask for advice are perceived by others as more self-confident.

Don't hide in a team. The often-cited Pareto Principle holds that 80% of the work is completed by 20% of the team. This principle likely explains the grousing by team members about those who don't pull their weight. The performance of any team you're on will reflect on you so, to the extent you can, choose your teammates carefully and ensure that the team project is a success. You may need to do more than your part.

Don't refer people or businesses lightly. Their performance following your endorsement reflects on your judgment. Decline a referral fee to avoid any appearance of a conflict of interest.

Don't worry about internal competitors. Just be your best self, do your best work, and trust that rationality will prevail. What more can you do? You're certainly not going to engage in sabotage of any sort. Right?! Things have a way of working out, perhaps in unexpected ways better than you hoped.

Keep up with the world outside work. Before meetings begin, the conversation often turns to sports, movies, music, fashion, pop culture. And just maybe the stock market, the economy, and world news. Being conversant in these topics helps add to your pizzazz.

Excel at something outside work. Primarily because it makes life more interesting and fun. The side benefit is that the activity demonstrates your discipline, focus, and competence. Word may get around that you're accomplished both at and outside work.

> *In my day it helped to excel at golf (which I didn't play) because business was discussed and camaraderie was developed between team members during these outings. Regardless of your athletic ability, have you some skill or talent that might help you gain exposure where you work? Perhaps excelling at cornhole, tossing darts (now axes), or playing pool. Or singing karaoke—"Sweet Caroline, oh, oh, oh!"*

Write!

CHAPTER TWO

"It's none of their business that you have to learn to write.
Let them think you were born that way."

ERNEST HEMINGWAY, NOVELIST AND JOURNALIST

Write

Your ability to use the written word will play a large role in determining your effectiveness and overall career trajectory. Your readers have too much to do and too little time to make sense of fuzzy thinking or bad grammar. They need writing that promotes understanding, sound decisions, and action. You write for many reasons, but in its highest form you write to persuade—to influence the opinion of others, including their opinion of you.

A survey of executives at 120 major American corporations employing nearly eight million people found that writing is a "threshold skill" for both employment and promotion of salaried employees. Executives emphasized, "Writing ability could be your ticket in . . . or it could be your ticket out," "All employees must have writing ability," and "You can't move up without writing skills."

Similarly, another major study found that "Written Communication" skill is "very important" to 93% of employers. Consulting guru Peter Drucker explains why: "As soon as you move one step up from the bottom, your effectiveness depends on your ability to reach others through the spoken or the written word . . . The letter, the report or memorandum, the ten-minute spoken 'presentation' to a committee are basic tools of the employee . . . This ability to express yourself is perhaps the most important of all the skills you can possess."

> *Some contend that writing is becoming the most sought-after skill in the job market, with historically underemployed English majors being increasingly favored in the hiring process. If so, it's about damn time!*

The higher you go, the more your writing ability matters. You'll be held to a higher standard because your writing will be seen by more people, and because you'll be editing the writing of others. To add to the stakes, the written word has an indefinite shelf life. Your writing may be read now and years from now, by intended and unintended parties. All will form an impression of you based on what they read.

You might believe you're already a skilled writer. After all, you've been writing a long time. You're not alone—many of us think we're skilled writers, just like we think we're great drivers. How odd, then, that a study conducted by the College Board concludes that one-third of employees do not meet the writing requirements of their jobs. An executive with the ManpowerGroup, a Fortune 500 staffing agency, suggests what's causing the problem: "With Gen X and Gen Y, because everything is shorthand and text, the ability to communicate effectively is challenged. You see it in the business world, whether with existing employees or job candidates."

> *After law school, I served as law clerk for a judge serving on the Supreme Court of North Carolina. I drafted legal opinions that, after editing by the judge, became law of the state. Surely, I was hot stuff. Not exactly. One could barely see what I wrote through all the red ink, opinion after opinion, month after month. Finally, when departing after my one-year clerkship, the judge informed me that from now on his clerks would serve two years. "Because I was so good you hate to lose me?" His reply: "No, because by the time you were any good, you were leaving."*

With few exceptions, those at the top know how to write and know good writing when they see it. They expect their people to write well. That many people don't write well, while thinking they do, poses an opportunity for you—but only if you agree that your writing skill matters and that you have room for improvement. Each writing assignment is an opportunity to show that you're a competent writer and a valuable member of your organization.

What follows in this chapter addresses the most common problems we see with the business writing of young professionals. Learn and apply the prin-

ciples that follow to make noticeable improvement in your business writing. Assuming you have something to say—substantive, well-conceived thoughts that add value to your reader—your message will have impact and reflect well on you wherever it travels. You'll be the exception by delivering writing that is clear, concise, and correct.

My first boss out of law school lamented the lack of writing skills of law school graduates. Poor writing by otherwise smart business types created legal work for our firm and helped me pay bar tabs and bulldog Frank's vet bills.

WRITE ROADMAP

Be Clear

1. Have a Plan
2. Keep It Simple
3. Make It Powerful

Be Concise

1. Nix the Nonsense
2. Lose the Modifier
3. Eliminate Excess Words

Be Correct

1. Strive for Perfection
2. Choose the Right Word
3. Arrange Words Properly

Be Clear

Clear writing is the first step to effective writing. Determine what you want to say, how to say it, and what to omit. Make your writing easy for your reader to understand. Here's how:

1. Have a Plan

Determine why you're writing. Take the time to think and plan before you start writing. Often job-related writing pertains to sharing information or calling for action, or a combination of both. Start by asking yourself: Who

is my audience? What do I want them to know? And what do I want them to do?

Consider mapping out your ideas before writing. Identify the most important information to place at the beginning of the document. For longer or more complex documents, brainstorm ideas and cluster similar ideas together. Then, decide on the order by numbering the ideas.

This planning process doesn't always work, or works but only so far. Sometimes I start writing to discover what it is I think I want to say. If stuck, just start writing and see if your thoughts evolve as you go.

Devise your structure. Decide how to best structure your document using a logical progression. Consider structuring in threes. Aristotle taught the power of writing and speaking in threes to promote understanding, retention, and action. Three things are easy to take in and to remember. Once you start looking for this device, you'll see that the power of threes is used frequently by authors and speakers.

Veni, vidi, vici. Body, mind, soul. Good, better, best. The three-act structure of a play, movie, or other source of narrative fiction, such as A Christmas Carol *by Charles Dickens, with Ghosts of Christmas Past, Present, and Future.*

Perhaps you can borrow from a well-executed company document that suggests your structure. Play with different structures until you have one that works well.

Start strong. Begin your business documents with your purpose for writing and, where applicable, the issue to be decided and your recommendation. Your reader will then know at the outset why you're writing and the action you recommend. If your document is longer than two or three pages, consider starting with an Executive Summary.

> *A properly done executive summary could stand alone if the reader stopped reading. It briefly states the issue to be decided, your recommendation, and your reasons. The longer your document, the longer the executive summary, since it must include the major points of the document.*

Write newspaper style. Put your most important material first. Newspaper editors say, "Don't bury the lead," meaning that the title and beginning paragraphs of a newspaper story should convey the gist of the news, with the detail following. Most readers never "turn to page 7A" where the story continues because they've read all they want to know. Contrast this approach with "magazine style," where the story builds to its climax. Says hedge fund manager Paul Tudor Jones, "Every time I get a memo from someone written magazine style, I literally tear it up, throw it away, and make them take an online newspaper writing course."

So write in a hierarchical way, with information included in the order of its importance in the document. The main points should be at the beginning of the document and the beginning of each section. Within paragraphs, put the most important material first and then provide detail. Each paragraph expresses one primary idea—the first sentence introduces the idea and the remaining sentences support it.

> *If texting parents or friends to tell them you've been in a plane crash or picked up by the Turkish police, your lead, if accurate, is "I'm fine."*

Make an exception to hierarchical writing when, say, you're delivering bad news, and you want to build a case to prepare the reader for a soft landing.

End strong. After you make your argument, end with your recommendation. If you're giving me—the reader—information, tell me why I need to know it, what I am to do with it, and by when. If you're asking or suggesting that I do something, what are the action steps you want me to take? End with what, in your view, are the next steps.

Write, edit, marinate. Once you start writing, let the words flow. Writing and editing are different processes, so don't stop to edit as you write. It's much more effective, and faster, if you resist the urge to edit until your thoughts are

captured on screen or paper, ready to revise. For larger writing projects, allow time for your thoughts to marinate between edits. You can only make so many changes at a time. Write, edit, let it sit, and then come back to it later. Your document will benefit from your refreshed perspective, and you'll then see changes to make that you don't see now.

2. Keep It Simple

As Mark Twain (real name Samuel Clemens) wrote to a friend, "I notice that you use plain, simple language, short words and brief sentences. That is the way to write English . . . Stick to it. Don't let fluff and flowers and verbosity creep in." To write clearly, keep it simple.

Write short sentences. Sometimes long sentences are necessary to express complex ideas. Given, however, the clauses, qualifiers, and parentheticals they require, long sentences may tax the memory and confuse your reader. Short sentences are easier to understand, so whenever possible prefer them. And so:

- Try to limit sentences to one or two (max) lines.
- If a sentence has lots of commas, rework to simplify it.
- Break up long sentences into clauses using (a), (b), (c) or (i), (ii), (iii).
- Combine short sentences if they sound choppy.

To help the reader stay awake, I try to avoid more than two long sentences in a row. I also like to mix in some one- or two-word sentence fragments. I realize grammarians would put me in the penalty box for doing this. I use them anyway, judiciously, for interest and emphasis.

Write short paragraphs. Long paragraphs are intimidating and annoying. It's hard to define when a paragraph is too long, but readers know it when they see it. If in doubt whether your paragraph is too long, it probably is. Rewrite it to either shorten or turn it into more than one paragraph.

Do lists right. Lists of numbered or bulleted items are a terrific tool to break your content into digestible, bite-size pieces. Done right—and not as a lengthy, random string of items—a list is a gift to the reader since it economizes words. Sometimes an entire document can be a list, as with an agenda. To use bullets effectively:

- Start each bullet with a verb (if possible).
- Use parallel construction (same form and tense of first word).
- Group similar items, and use subheadings if the list is long.

- List the items in an intentional order, such as most to least important, the order of steps to be taken, the chronology.
- Put a period at the end of each bullet, or not, but be consistent.

Technically, a period is required when a bullet is a complete sentence. If you're consistent, whatever you do will go unnoticed—and be fine—for business writing.

When should you list items using numbers verses bullets? Use numbers to signal that the sequence of listed items is important to follow, as in numbered steps in a process.

Fix vague references. People unintentionally use vague references when they speak as well as write. A vague reference is often a pronoun such as *her, him, she, he, it, their, them, they, we, who,* or *who's* that confuses the reader because the noun to which the pronoun is referring isn't clear. The reader (or listener) can't identify to whom or to what you're referring.

"The contract calls for Maytag to replace the washers every ten years. A local vendor, Suds n' Duds, offers a greater revenue share, but will not commit to replace the washers. Both appear reliable. I believe *they* are the right choice."

Who is *they*? The vague reference guts the point of the recommendation. Fix the vague reference by providing the missing name. And so: "I believe Maytag is the right choice."

Or, "Joyce will be presenting the proposal to the client, and most likely to Susan, the CEO, and it is critical that *she* understand the nuances of our pricing structure." The reader wonders (or the listener asks), "Who is *she*?" Sometimes the identity of the vague reference is not found within the sentence: "The department is not performing as expected." Which department? Once again, avoid the vague reference by providing the name. You don't need to name the subject every time, just when needed to ensure clarity.

Clarify acronyms. When you use an acronym for the first time, show what the letters stand for. Write the full term in your text, then put the acronym in quotes within parentheses immediately following:

- The projected initial year Return on Investment ("ROI") is 7.5%.
- The Initial Public Offering ("IPO") will launch in April.
- The Executive Committee ("EC") meets quarterly.

Now the reader will know your meaning when you use the acronym later in your text. Only define terms when you use the acronym again; otherwise, there's no need to do so.

Use the same word when you mean the same thing. Some of us were taught to add variety and interest to our writing by using different words or synonyms when we mean the same thing. Known as elegant variation, this is bad advice for business writing. Repeat the same word when you mean the same thing, no matter how many times it appears. Otherwise, your reader might misunderstand you, assuming your shift in word choice signals a shift in meaning.

> "The use fee shall be 1% of Franchisee's gross revenue. Franchise payments shall be made on or before the 5th day of each month."

Say what? Is the "use fee" something different than a "franchise payment"? If so, when must the use fee be paid, and how much is the franchise payment?

And so, don't interchange offer, initial proposal, and opening bid. Or deadline, time constraint, and time for completion. Or case, matter, and dispute.

3. Make It Powerful

Use base verbs. Verbs are your action words, and every complete sentence must have one. They give your writing punch, especially when you use the base form of the verb. The base verb is the verb in its purest form, without an ending such as *-ed*, *-ing*, *-ion* or *-s*. For example, the base verb is "persuade" rather than "persuaded," "persuading," "persuasion," or "persuades." Which verb form has more punch?

- take action . . . act
- make a decision . . . decide
- make a statement . . . state
- are supportive of . . . support
- give authorization . . . authorize
- draw a conclusion . . . conclude

Base verbs are simple, clear, and powerful. Shorten your verbs until you find the base verb.

Be Concise

Now that your writing is clear—structured, simple, and powerful—let's tighten it further by using as few words as possible. While clarity should not be sacrificed for brevity, write concisely to help ensure your writing gets read,

and to promote understanding and action. Many business executives view reading memos, reports, and emails as a distraction from the real work of the business. They read because it's their job to do so, but they don't appreciate those who prolong this distraction with needless verbiage.

> *At one of my jobs, I was told to keep all memos short because the head honcho wouldn't read anything longer than one page. This rumor was untrue, but the advice was solid. He viewed reading long documents as a poor use of his time. He had people like me to do grunt work.*

To streamline your writing, strike whole lines, shorten phrases, and turn phrases into single words. Cut words that add nothing, dilute your message, or make your reader work. If you cut three to five words from a sentence, the result is eighteen to thirty fewer words in a six-sentence paragraph. Be relentless—every word you cut matters, and the cumulative effect will make a profound difference in your writing. Work to recognize verbosity and to fix it.

1. Nix the Nonsense

Cut business buzzwords. You won't differentiate your writing with pretentious mumbo-jumbo that says nothing, inhibits clarity, and induces eye rolling. Spare your reader words and clichés such as empower, platform, proactive, outside the box, and synergy. And paradigm (always "shifting").

> *String buzzwords together, and you get authentic business gibberish: "We are proactively breaking down silos to integrate horizontal change." "We are recontextualizing core processes to leverage impactful disruption." "We are pivoting across organic boundaries to synthesize process ownership." Lose the buzzwords when writing (and speaking) and say what you mean in plain words.*

Cut garbage phrases. Writers (and speakers) begin sentences with pompous-sounding phrases that mean nothing and take up space. Phrases such as:

- I might add
- I should point out
- it's important to add

- it goes without saying
- it is interesting to note
- if I'm not mistaken

If something is "important to add," just add it. If something "goes without saying," then why write (or say) it? If you assert that something is "interesting to note," you challenge your reader to find it uninteresting (just as beginning a story or joke with "this is funny" challenges your audience to find it lame). Let your audience be the judge, finding it interesting (or funny) on their own.

Cut unsupported claims. "Our company boasts the most talented, hardworking, service-oriented people in the business." Really? What business is that? Has the company made a comprehensive study to back up this claim? Easy to write, but such a grandiose claim in a competitive industry requires proof. Or this, from a pitch piece: "We provide unparalleled value to others in our dedication to excellent results, attention to details, and delivering a working environment of mutual respect and unsurpassed integrity." Prove it with data, with testimonials, with something. Or don't say it.

2. Lose the Modifier

A modifier is a word that comes before the most important word and adds information about it. You needn't concern yourself with whether the modifier is an adverb, adjective, noun, or something else. You need only recognize surplus words so you can cut them or, better still, not write them in the first place. Most modifiers are surplus words. They take up space, make the modified word less powerful, and render your writing clichéd and hyperbolic.

Use modifiers sparingly. Eliminate modifiers such as:

- *completely* agree . . . agree
- *firmly* believe . . . believe
- *fully* protected . . . protected
- *overly* dramatic . . . dramatic
- *safely* assume . . . assume
- *very* compelling . . . compelling

Mark Twain explains why: "God only exhibits his thunder and lightning at intervals, and so they always command attention . . . You thunder and lightning too much; the reader ceases to get under the bed, by and by." Losing the modifier results in understatement—the right tone for business writing—and brings a calmness and appearance of considered thought to your writing. Modifiers that remain are more powerful due to their scarcity.

See if your word works fine on its own, without the modifier. It almost always will. *Clearly, really, simply, totally*, and *very* are obvious cuts. Twain suggests, "Substitute *damn* every time you're inclined to write *very*; your editor will delete it and the writing will be just as it should be."

Don't use conflicting modifiers. Unless you're trying to be humorous by using words that don't go together, don't use modifiers such as:

- *fairly* toxic
- *pretty* shocking
- *rather* catastrophic
- *slightly* hysterical
- *somewhat* terrified
- *mostly* dead

Substitute a stronger word instead of a modifier. Such as:

- extremely busy . . . swamped
- much confusion . . . chaos
- quite puzzling . . . baffling
- very angry . . . enraged
- very sad . . . morose
- very tired . . . exhausted

A modifier we find useful when disagreeing or offering an alternate view is "respectfully." If the words and tone that follow are indeed respectful, "respectfully submit" sets a deferential tone. As does "respectfully contend" or "respectfully request."

> In contrast, the phrase "with all due respect" is inevitably followed by statements that are not respectful; its use signals an attack and hence should not be used.

3. Eliminate Excess Words

Excess words represent your greatest opportunity to streamline your writing, but are more difficult to spot and fix than buzzwords, garbage phases, and modifiers. Fixing excess words usually involves rewriting.

Spot suspect words. Suspect words are often part of clauses that can be trimmed to shorten your sentences. Learn to spot these verbose word clusters and then rewrite:

Case—in case, many cases, most cases
- *In most cases* the parts are in the box
 - Usually the parts are in the box

Instance—some instances, majority of instances, there was an instance
- *This is an instance when* it would have been better to
 - Here, it would have been better to

Fact—the fact that
- *Because of the fact that* more accidents have happened
 - Because more accidents have happened

There—there is, there are, there was, there were, there can, there had
- *It is evident there is* a morale issue in your department
 - Your department has a morale issue

That—that are, that is, that the, that there, that was, that were, that can, that had
- *It is clear that there are* too many people in the accounting department
 - The accounting department has too many people

Who—who is, who are, who was, who were, who can, who had
- *Anyone who is a* candidate for employment must pass a physical exam
 - Anyone seeking employment must pass a physical exam

Which—which is, which are, which was, which were, which can, which had
- Our competitor visiting the prospect, when we did not, *was a fact which had* a material effect on us losing the business.
 - Our failure to visit the prospect was important in our losing the business

Try eliminating the word "the" whenever you can. See how your sentence reads without it. "She has *the* potential to be a rising star at the firm" becomes "She has potential to be a rising star at the firm."

Trim wordy phrases. They're everywhere! Shorten as follows:

- at a later date . . . later
- at such time as . . . when
- for the purpose of . . . to
- in order to . . . to
- in regard to . . . regarding
- in the event of . . . if

Up for a challenge? See if you can reduce this twenty-two-word sentence to nine words: "In many instances, as far as prospects are concerned, the lease terms are not understandable because they are written in lawyer jargon." One solution: "Often lawyer jargon prevents prospects from understanding lease terms."

Watch for words that say the same thing. Shorten phrases that say or imply the same thing by losing one of the words and making the other do the work:

- advanced planning . . . planning
- basic fundamentals . . . basics
- close proximity . . . close
- past experience . . . experience
- same exact . . . same
- end result . . . result

Writing concisely—cutting, rearranging, improving—is a skill that, like any other, takes practice to develop. Once you have on paper (or screen) what you want to say, review your draft to identify surplus words and revise to write tighter, reader-friendly sentences. As said by Supreme Court Justice Louis Brandeis, "There is no great writing, only great rewriting."

Call me eccentric (or worse), but when I see a paragraph ending with a line of just a few words, I consider it a challenge to rewrite the paragraph to eliminate that last dangling snippet of a line. There's always a way to do it—and the revision is better.

I have OCD tendencies, but this is too much even for me.

Your writing will improve—guaranteed!—if you apply these teachings. You're getting the idea when you ask, "How can I make this sentence shorter and tighter?" Then, once you spot the wordiness, cut excess words. Eventually the process will go faster because you'll recognize wordiness as you write, so you won't need to cut so many words when you rewrite.

Be Correct

Once you have a solid draft that is both clear and concise, you can now perfect it.

Some companies have a style guide laying out their standards for workplace writing. In the unlikely event your company has one, follow its standards. More important, write how your manager wants you to write, even if her way conflicts with some style guide. Learn from her edits so you don't annoy your manager by triggering the same old corrections. Depending on your manager, you may never get a document back with no edits, but over time you should see less red ink.

Most bosses have writing-related pet peeves. Some of mine:

- *Documents and exhibits not formatted to print (some of us still print!)—assume your document will be printed, so format it.*
- *Unnumbered pages—if the printer spews your document on the floor, or if I drop it, don't make me try to reconstruct the order of pages.*
- *Unconsolidated attachments—I don't consider opening a boatload of attachments to be a good use of my time.*
- *Using different words in the Table of Contents or a List of Exhibits from those in the corresponding text headers or exhibit titles—don't make me guess where I am in your document or whether I'm looking at the exhibit you referenced.*

1. Strive for Perfection

Strive to perfect your spelling, punctuation, and grammar. You won't literally be perfect (nor are we in writing *Look Out Above!*), but set a high bar for yourself. Here are solutions to common business writing mistakes we see, using a "Top Ten List" format from least to most important.

10. Purge the inappropriate, immature, and informal. This includes profanity, emojis (☺), and texting-style abbreviations (bcoz, btw, bz, g1, OMG, thx, TL:DR, u), as well as BHOF if referring to the senior author here. If your boss does any of this (LOL), that's his prerogative. If you absolutely must use emojis, wait until you're the boss to do so!

9. Limit your use of contractions. While formerly taboo, the use of contractions in casual emails and texts is now acceptable. Consider both the nature of the document and the audience. When the document needs a more formal tone, or when writing to your manager, clients, or prospective clients, use contractions sparingly. Limit contractions to informal documents written to peers.

8. Use an apostrophe when you mean "it is" or "it has." Conversely, use "its" when you don't mean "it is" or "it has." And so, "it's a beautiful day," and "the store is having its going out of business sale" are both correct. "Thank God its Friday" is incorrect.

7. Avoid colloquialisms unique to your locale. Here in North Carolina, people say "hankering," "rassle," and "y'all." Only a goober lets such local expressions creep into his business writing. Since you don't know where or how far your writing will travel, avoid colloquialisms that may mean something different to the reader than you intended.

> *The phrase "bless his (or her) heart" is a Southern way of cloaking an insult in politeness. Put more succinctly by the Urban Dictionary, it's "the most Southern f**k you" there is. When I hear "bless his heart," I rub my hands together in giddy anticipation, as I know the speaker is about to unload on someone.*

6. Prefer the active to the passive voice. The *active voice* emphasizes who is doing the doing, usually by placing the subject before the verb. The *passive voice* doesn't emphasize who is doing the doing, and the subject, if any, is usually placed after the verb. Prefer the active voice because it makes clear who is doing what to whom, and because it uses fewer words. When the passive voice dominates a document, it becomes tedious to read and may make the reader search for a subject. To illustrate:

- Passive: A complaint was filed by the customer.
- Active: The customer filed a complaint.
- Passive: The order was placed by our marketing department.
- Active: Our marketing department placed the order.

Sometimes the passive voice has no subject:

- A complaint was filed.
- The order was placed.
- It is suspected that.

Who filed the complaint, placed the order, or suspects? The reader doesn't know because the actor is hidden. "The feeling is that you're not the right fit for the role." Who feels that way? The primary business use of the passive voice is to duck ownership. "The data was lost." "The contract was signed without authority." "The goal was not achieved." Not the right approach if it was you who screwed up!

5. Properly set off quotes inside a sentence. Capitalize the first word in a complete quotation, even in midsentence:

- Holmes replied, "Elementary, my dear Watson."
- King Longshanks observed, "I don't want my head in a basket."
- The Don counseled, "Never tell anyone outside the family what you're thinking again."

Don't capitalize quoted material if it continues a sentence:

- Holmes exclaimed that the "game is afoot."
- Unbeknownst to his son, the king had "already made plans."
- Clemenza told Rocco to "leave the gun" but "take the cannoli."

As shown above, use a comma before the quote to set off complete quotations, and to introduce or interrupt quotations. Otherwise, you don't need one.

4. Put quotation marks in the right place. Periods and commas go inside quotation marks. All other punctuation marks go outside of the quotation marks unless they are part of the quote itself. And so:

- No: One of our company's core values is "Continuous Improvement".
- Yes: One of our company's core values is "Continuous Improvement."

- No: In addition to "Continuous Improvement", other core values are . . .
- Yes: In addition to "Continuous Improvement," other core values are . . .

Apparently, the Brits put periods and commas outside of quotation marks. Unless you're in the London office, do it the stateside way. And spare your reader pretentious (in this country) spellings such as "theatre" for theater, "centre" for center and "colour" for color. But, speaking of color, feel free to substitute "bollocks" for balls.

3. Master the serial (aka *Oxford* or *Harvard*) comma. The serial comma is the final comma (or not) in a list of things. For example: "Dean Wormer counseled Bluto not to go through life drunk, fat, and stupid." The serial comma is the one after the word "fat." Some style guides insist the comma be added; others say it's fine to omit the serial comma when doing so doesn't create a confusing sentence. Deleting the final comma to read "drunk, fat and stupid" works fine.

Here's advocating that you always include the serial comma. Doing so promotes a consistent style, saves you from deciding what to do on a comma-by-comma basis, and ensures clarity. It also spares the reader from wondering why sometimes you added that last comma and sometimes you left it out. Ignore spell-check if it prompts you to remove the serial comma. For the same reasons, we suggest adding the serial comma if the final item is preceded by "or" instead of "and."

2. Conform singular and plural references. A pronoun referring to something earlier in the text (its antecedent) must agree in number—singular or plural—with the antecedent. This sentence is flawed: "Look at what a job candidate has done to reveal what they can do." "Job candidate" is singular; "they" is plural. Make both the pronoun and the antecedent plural ("Look at what job candidates have done") or make both singular ("to reveal what he or she can do"). The culprit is often a mismatched "they" or "them" when referencing a singular pronoun such as anyone, everyone, someone, no one, and nobody.

1. Eliminate typos. Not catching typos is sloppy, and as typos accumulate they suggest you didn't bother or don't know how to proofread. Develop a disdain for typos and ferret them out. Whatever editing technique you use, whether pen-to-paper or on-screen, challenge yourself starting now to make every written communication you send flawless. Proof every document, email, and text before sending.

While not practical for emails and texts, editing pen-to-paper is the only way, in my view, for you to achieve the error-free spelling, punctuation, and grammar required, as well as the clarity and brevity previously discussed. For documents you consider important (your own or those of others that you're editing), I recommend you first edit on screen, then print and edit again on paper.

I'll disagree, and counter that editing on screen is effective, time-saving, and better for the environment. It's an acquired skill, and one worth acquiring. By my estimate, 95% of Look Out Above! *was edited on screen.*

Perhaps try this. Edit your next few documents on screen until, in your view, the document is perfect, then print to see whether you discover more edits and opportunities to improve. If with practice you can do what Nick suggests, more power to you.

2. Choose the Right Word

First, play defense. Don't confuse words having (1) the identical sound, (2) a similar sound, or (3) a close but different meaning. And don't use sexist words. In each of these scenarios, Spell Check won't help since your incorrect or sexist word choice is spelled correctly.

Beware of words with identical sounds, especially when dictating. Otherwise, you may appear to be an uneducated buffoon:

- cite . . . site
- eminent . . . imminent
- here . . . hear
- our . . . are
- principal . . . principle
- there . . . their . . . they're

An investment package we received described the valet trash service provided to residents under the heading "Waist Management." Not the right impression to give when seeking to raise millions of dollars. Solution: proof your work. Misused words can cause unintended laughs at your expense.

Beware of words with similar sounds. A malapropism is the mistaken use of a word in place of a similar-sounding one, sometimes with unintended humorous effect:

- child progeny (prodigy)
- an allusion (illusion) of integrity
- pigment (figment) of my imagination
- a suppository (repository) of information
- illiterate (obliterate) him from your memory
- thank you for your copulation (cooperation)

> *I received a letter from my health insurance provider apologizing for any "incontinence" that their billing error had caused. Yes, the error was inconvenient, but it didn't cause me to lose bowel control.*

Solution: choose the right word by building your vocabulary and proofing your work!

Beware of words with close but different meaning. Danger lurks here:

- affect . . . effect
- comprise . . . compose
- continual . . . continuous
- criteria . . . criterion
- farther . . . further
- implied . . . inferred

When in doubt, consult an online dictionary to identify the correct word. Otherwise, choose another word. Like this:

- Betty implied from my email that I did not support the deal (incorrect word)
 - Betty inferred from my email that I did not support the deal (correct word)
 - Betty concluded from my email that I did not support the deal (substitute word)

There's always another word that substitutes nicely, and it's never been easier to go online to find the correct use of a word or a synonym (or to check your grammar usage).

Reframe sexist words. Sexist words suggest to the reader you're a misogynist, a Neanderthal, or both. When referring to a named individual, use of the corresponding he or she, or him or her, is fine. Otherwise:

Don't use expressions that imply value judgments based on sex:

- She lost the account, but took it like a man.
- That property is the weak sister of the portfolio.
- He's a girly-man.

Don't use sex-based descriptions and titles:

- Workman's compensation (worker's compensation)
- Reasonable man (reasonable person)
- Dick/bitch (challenging personality)

Don't use non-parallel constructions when referring to both sexes:

- Men and their wives (men and women, or husbands and wives)
- Ladies and men (ladies and gentlemen, or women and men)
- All sexes welcome (choose any bathroom you like!)

Don't use "he" or "him" as a reference:

- The average resident pays his rent on time (Most residents pay rent on time).
- Each executive must think for himself (Executives must think for themselves).
- Every volunteer knows he has done something worthwhile (All volunteers know they have done something worthwhile).

Bottom line: write around sexist writing. There's always a way.

Use familiar words. You played defense by not choosing an incorrect word. Now play offense by choosing the best word. Usually it's the shorter and more familiar word. William Faulkner wrote that Ernest Hemingway "has never been known to use a word that might send a reader to the dictionary." For business writing, that's a good thing!

If choosing between the writing style of Hemingway and that of Faulkner, choose the former. While acknowledging Faulkner's luminary/legendary/badass status, I have yet to finish one of his novels, and I've tried at least a dozen times. Sentences that run on for pages are not my idea of a good read. If you want to see familiar words in action, try Hemingway's "The Short Happy Life of Francis Macomber."

According to one study, people who dress up their writing with long, complicated words are perceived as *less* intelligent by readers. In a recent sports page article about the local hockey team, the columnist used the word "defenestration." We doubt many fans knew that one! Choose familiar words likely to be understood by your reader, rather than pompous words showing how erudite, sagacious, and perspicacious you are. Don't use "commence" for "begin," "propitious" for "favorable," or "utilize" for "use." Aristotle once again is spot on: "Clearness is secured by using words . . . that are current and ordinary."

For 3rd grade Back-to-School night, son Will was required to complete an "All About Me" worksheet for parental consumption on the bulletin board. One question was, "What do you want to be when you grow up?" Will wanted to be a sportscaster. Older brother Nick told him to use a "fancier" word—sure to impress—that meant the same thing. The word? "Proctologist." My wife Jane and I got some weird looks.

He was so sweet and trusting. It was too easy.

Find the best word. Use a longer or less familiar word when the word is (1) precise, with no better substitutes to express your meaning and tone, (2) economical, such that a longer word saves using multiple smaller words, or (3) perfect, because the word is funny or ironic, suggests a desired subtlety, sets the mood, or has a special meaning to your reader.

Having a robust vocabulary is required for avoiding mistakes and finding the best word. The more words you know, the more likely you can summon the word you want. Being able to do so makes your writing more interesting for the reader and more fun for you. In a time when the average person's vocab-

ulary was 700 words, Shakespeare's topped 21,000. Can you find the right word when needed?

If you're up for the challenge, list "vocabulary" as an interest on your résumé. While doing so is a "kick-me" invitation and may elicit a few test words in a job interview, vocabulary is an interest few others will list, and word power directly pertains to communication skills and work success.

If you need more convincing to build your word power, consider: A graduating class at a large university was given a vocabulary exam. The scores were graded in 5% quantiles. Throughout the next twenty years, questionnaires were sent to the graduates asking them, among other items, their income. Those who had scored in the top 5% on the vocabulary test consistently had the highest incomes, and those who scored in the bottom 5% had the lowest incomes.

Studies show vocab-building activities to be good for long-term brain health. I have an iPhone app that sends me a new vocabulary word every day at 7:30 am. If it's a particularly tasty word, I'll screenshot it and keep the screenshot until I've incorporated the word into my vocabulary.

3. Arrange Words Properly

Keep in mind three rules for arranging your word order:

Shrink the gaps between related words. Put related words close together. The intended meaning of the following sentences is clarified by placing the words that relate to each other closer together (both shown in italics):

- I will *discuss* with Jon how and when to inform Steve *tomorrow*.
 - I will *discuss* with Jon *tomorrow* how and when to inform Steve.

- My supervisor *discussed* your proposal to drain the swamp *with his partners*.
 - My supervisor *discussed with his partners* your proposal to drain the swamp.

- Due to his *goofy temperament and gas* my friends always laugh at my *bulldog.*
 - My friends always laugh at my *bulldog's goofy temperament and gas.*

Shrink the gaps between related concepts. Similarly, don't make the reader leap across explanatory material to connect the concepts:

- *The contract*, unless earlier revoked by either party, *will expire on January 15.*
 - *The contract will expire on January 15*, unless earlier revoked by either party.

- If interested, *contact a registered agent* to discuss the contract *by March 1.*
 - If interested, *contact a registered agent by March 1* to discuss the contract.

- *Begin*, before discussing our fee and timing of first payment, *by emphasizing how our service network and response time will benefit them.*
 - *Begin by emphasizing how our service network and response time will benefit them*, before discussing our fee and timing of first payment.

Place the word to be emphasized at the end of a sentence. What is said last is remembered most. Next best is to start with it. Don't bury the word to be emphasized in the middle.

- Worst: By all accounts a *horse's ass* is what he is.
- Better: A *horse's ass* is what he is by all accounts.
- Best: By all accounts he's a *horse's ass.*

Conclusion

Clear, concise, and correct—your keys to powerful business writing.

Take pride in everything you write. If you remember nothing else from this chapter, write short sentences, use strong verbs, and use as few words as possible. Twain notes, "A wordy, diffuse, flowery habit, once fastened upon a person, is as hard to get rid of as any other vice." Maybe so, but you can get better with practice. As your skills progress, and your confidence grows, you may find you enjoy writing more (or dislike it less). You may even get great feedback from your boss and, better still, she may ask you to take a look at her prose.

Application: Emails

Your emails give readers a glimpse into your personality, writing skill, work habits, and, if you let them, your stress level. Perhaps, too, your workplace status. A person's level in an organization can often be discerned by reading her emails. Emails written by those in the lower echelons tend to be too casual in tone, with abbreviations and slang. Those nearer the top write emails as they would a memorandum to their manager, with a formal tone, good grammar, and proper punctuation. Senior executives expect their people to write proper emails.

Big Picture

Apply the clear, concise, and correct principles of Look Out Above! *to every email.* Then proofread—carefully.

Use your work email for business emails only. Send or forward (if you must) on your own time jokes, memes, political rants, patriotic mishmash, and videos of your dog. And use a personal email account.

Don't send an email when a conversation is called for. Any email that exceeds a couple of long paragraphs suggests a conversation may be more effective—pick up the phone or walk down the hall. Conversely, don't call for a meeting when a quick email would suffice.

Adhere to email conventions at your company. Follow conventions regarding use of out-of-office messages, response time to emails, and anything else.

> *Since typos are more likely to occur when thumbing email replies on your phone, consider adding a standard message at the conclusion that says "Sent from my mobile device. Please pardon typos." If dictating emails using Siri or her ilk, beware. She once translated my message "Good luck in the boardroom" to "Good luck in the bathroom."*

Don't write anything you don't want forwarded. You don't know where your email is going (maybe even to your file in Human Resources). You can ask the recipients not to forward, but you can't control or know what they do. Don't write things that don't show you at your best or that you don't want unintended parties to read. Rewrite or delete but don't send.

Delay replying to an offensive email. Write your reply and save it as a draft, but don't send until you've calmed down and are thinking rationally. If you can sleep on it, all the better. "Flaming" emails written late at night when you're tired, or in ALL CAPS BECAUSE YOU'RE ANGRY, are unlikely to help and reflect poorly on you. Your delay in responding may suggest to the sender—and rightly so—that the email you received was inappropriate, requiring a considered response.

Sometimes you won't have the luxury of time in crafting your response to an offensive email because a prompt reply is needed. If you have a mentor in the organization, consult him or her for advice. I have found advice from a trusted friend or colleague to be useful in "the heat of the moment," when I might write a slashing retort based on emotion rather than logic. If such a sounding board isn't available, at least step away from your email—get up, walk around, and clear your head before sending your response. Remind yourself that the offensive email sitting in your inbox is likely not personal, nor should be your response.

Don't use the email retract feature. Most people look at retracted emails more carefully than normal ones, to see what all the hubbub is about!

To, Cc, and Bcc

For important emails, type in recipient names and email addresses last. This precludes accidentally sending before you're ready.

Double-check the recipient list before you hit "Send." Especially check emails that include or attach sensitive information; sending emails to the wrong people is embarrassing and could cause greater problems.

*A construction contractor emailed his partner about me, and inadvertently copied me: "Did the little ****head even consider our proposal?" ****head? Little? Ouch!*

Send your emails only to necessary recipients. Pay attention to your "To" and "Cc" list. Is your email worth more clutter in the person's inbox? Don't "Reply All" when a "Reply" to the sender alone is all that's needed. Usually, for

example, following a company-wide announcement reply only to the applicable person. People don't need or want to know that you replied "Way to go!" about a new promotion. Likewise, a meeting organizer will send an email to multiple recipients asking about their availability to meet at certain times. Reply only to the sender; the other participants don't need or want to know the details of everyone's availability.

Use the blind carbon copy (Bcc) function for mass emails. Respect the privacy of recipients by not revealing their names or email addresses. Be mindful, too, of using "Reply All" when doing so inappropriately reveals the identity and email address of recipients.

Don't send Bccs to undisclosed recipients. Other than mass emails, the reader may reasonably assume the email went only to the recipients shown. If you send emails to undisclosed parties, and if this fact is discovered, you'll lose credibility. It's akin to not disclosing all parties present on a speakerphone call. If you know people who blind cc, then assume any email to you from them is also being sent to undisclosed recipients.

Subject Line, Launch, and Sign-Off

Create strong subject line headers that identify the purpose of the email. Include a strong verb when your email calls for action. If the email is time-sensitive, say so in the subject line.

Start your email text with the recipient's first name. Especially when you're emailing someone you don't regularly email, starting with his or her name adds a personal touch.

> *For a more personal touch, add the word "you" when appropriate. "It was good to meet" becomes "it was good to meet with you." "I look forward to meeting again" becomes "I look forward to meeting with you again."*

Don't clutter your email signature. Cut the inspirational quotes, goofy fonts, or, unless they pertain to your job, the dozen social media icons with links to your various social accounts.

Consider signing your emails with your initials. I end every email with my initials, rhs. Doing so isn't necessary to inform the recipient it's from me. So why do it? First, and most important, it says I own the email. I "signed" it. Second, it signals the end of the message, whether in the header or the text.

My brother Matt says the only emailers on the planet who do this are his father and father-in-law.

Content

Use good judgment. Be careful about what you put in writing, especially emails and texts, and be mindful of your language when you elect to write. Common sense dictates that you not write harmful emails that your company's lawyers will be compelled to disclose (your emails remain on the company's server even if you hit "delete"). You can act with integrity without creating a paper trail for opposing lawyers.

The following email was written by an employee of a company accused of stealing a competitor's design drawings and production schedules: "What we are doing is impossible for anyone to figure out. We know exactly what the other camp is doing. Sit back and enjoy the show . . . It is time to finish the job. By the time [they] realize what is happening, the game should be over." The game *was* over—for the writer of the email and his company. A $40 million jury verdict and bankruptcy followed.

Or this email, written by the head trainer of an NFL football team, who asked that a Drug Enforcement Agency certificate be faxed to him: "I need it for my records when the NFL 'pill counters' come to see if we are doing things right. Don't worry, I'm pretty good at keeping them off the trail!"

General Motors' lawyers, having had enough self-immolation, issued a do-not-use list of sixty-nine words to employees when writing or emailing about GM products. According to an article in the *Detroit Free Press*, this list included:

- Asphyxiating
- Deathtrap
- Disemboweling
- Grenadelike
- Powderkeg
- Widow-maker

The lawyers cautioned that writings should contain facts, and not speculations, opinions, or words with emotional connotations. While not executed well, the intent is understandable. Why would a company tolerate careless, inflammatory, or exaggerated language in internal communications?

Loose lips still sink ships—your company's, and yours. Choose your words carefully in emails and texts. Write your emails assuming disclosure to opposing counsel or newspaper readers. Don't write emails you would be embarrassed to explain. When in doubt, talk to someone in person.

Question and Answer

1. What's the proper tone for business writing?

Understated, and not casual or folksy. Identify your audience and, if mixed, make sure the tone is appropriate for the highest person in the chain. Simpler still is to write with the same formality to those both inside and outside your company.

Some pundits suggest to "write like you talk." What they mean, we think, is to use familiar words and short sentences that are easy to understand. But most of us speak as we think, and not in perfect sentences. And some of us repeat ourselves and speak w-a-a-a-y too much. Listeners may tolerate poor sentence construction, excess verbiage, and verbal diarrhea (see "Present"). Not so readers, who expect crisp writing. Writing allows time for reflection and revision that speaking does not, so readers afford less slack. Write better than you speak.

2. How do I respond when my supervisor edits my writing?

With tact and an open mind. The expression "It's always easier to edit than to write" is often meant as a kind remark to an author who took a stab at writing, but whose work was found wanting and edited beyond recognition. It *is* easier to edit than to write if the writing is well written and the edits are minimal. It's not easier to edit when the writing is a disaster. Then it's easier for the editor to start over and do the writing himself or herself. Or get someone else to do it.

> *When returning a writing assignment during my first year of law school, my professor—meaning to be encouraging, I think—assured me not to worry about my grade because "we couldn't all be English majors." I was an English major.*

Accept red ink, margin notes, and "rewrite!" with grace. Learn from reviewers' edits and comments. Your goal is less red ink with each successive draft and assignment. Learn what your supervisor wants and seek to write accordingly.

3. How do I respond when my supervisor asks me to edit her writing?

Recognize the opportunity to add value. Take the time to carefully review the document. Don't squander the opportunity by giving the document a quick review and saying, "It looks great." Consider the opportunity an honor and take it seriously. Earn the reputation of someone who gives thoughtful comments when asked to review a document. Look at its intended purpose and at whether that purpose is achieved. Look to see if you agree with the structure. Make sure the document follows a logical progression. Move paragraphs to the right place before you fix them, then fix broken sentences. Finally, catch every typo and make it correct.

Be mindful of how much you're changing. Don't impose your style or change words that work because you like another word better. And don't expect every change you propose to be adopted by the author. If you add value with your edits, you will earn gratitude and respect from whoever asked for your review. You helped them look, and be, better. Once your writing prowess and careful review of documents becomes known, your review will be sought on more important documents. That's a good thing!

4. Any final writing tips and tricks?

Don't start a sentence with "however." Rather than start a sentence with "however," put it after an initial clause to make the sentence more interesting. Not: "However, it is now apparent, he has no intention of paying us back." Instead: "It is now apparent, however, he has no intention of paying us back."

Be wary of starting a sentence with and, and so, as well, because, but, moreover, further, in addition. Try the sentence without these words to see whether they are superfluous.

Emphasize words sparingly. When you do, use italics or bold, and not ALL CAPS or <u>underline</u> (except for hyperlinks).

Don't randomly and improperly replace the word "and" with an ampersand. An ampersand (&) is not a substitute for "and" in text, headings, or titles. Limit its use to proper nouns like company names (e.g. Barnes & Noble), names that are abbreviations (AT&T), and inside tables where space is limited.

Avoid ending a sentence with a preposition. Even though doing so is now deemed proper, lots of baby boomers missed the memo and consider it poor grammar.

Go easy on exclamation points. Don't overuse!!! If you must imply that something is astonishing, restrain your excitement to only one exclamation point or question mark.

Avoid clichés and don't mix metaphors. Don't fall off a piece of cake or get something by hook or ladder or grab the bull by the balls. If you mix metaphors, you'll be a duck out of water.

Avoid using "etc." Using *etc.* (which means "and so forth") suggests you don't know or were too lazy to think of the rest of the list. Instead of *etc.*, use "include" or "including" when listing items to avoid the burden of thinking of and listing every item that might apply. "Hard conversations include those . . ."

Use dashes instead of commas to set off material. Use dashes when you want to emphasize something. Dashes are more emphatic than commas which, in turn, are more emphatic than parentheses. A noted grammarian says, "Dash but don't be rash," meaning don't overdo it.

Use analogies and similes. Promote understanding by comparing the current topic to another the reader would know. This is like that, because. Many people watch, play, or have played a sport, so sports analogies may work well. Know your audience, and make sure the analogy or simile makes the intended point.

Consider restating a negative as a positive. Doing so may make your sentence more powerful and shorter. Consider flipping like this:

- not uncommon . . . typical
- not unimportant . . . important
- not unlike . . . is like
- not unlimited . . . limited
- not unreasonable . . . reasonable
- not unrelated . . . related

Sometimes, however, you want to emphasize the negative, perhaps to warn. Such as "don't let your guard down," "don't jeopardize your career," and "don't lose focus." Or perhaps you want more nuance or understatement: "I am not unaware that we've been sued."

Consider these action steps. From easier to more challenging:

- Take the *Reader's Digest* vocabulary test while waiting for the doctor or dentist.
- Choose an app and sign up to receive an online word of the day.
- Do crossword puzzles and check out the answers to see the words you missed.
- Read a vocabulary book (any SAT or ACT vocabulary prep book works fine).
- Volunteer for a writing assignment at work and solicit feedback.
- Take an online journalism class.

Present!

CHAPTER THREE

"Thank you, thank you! Hey, what a crowd! You look great this morning . . . really, I mean that! Go on, give yourselves a hand! You know, a funny thing happened on the way to the library yesterday . . ."

CALVIN (BEST FRIEND OF HOBBES), TO HIS FIRST GRADE CLASS

Present

Chances are you've already done a presentation. By the time you've hit your twenties you've likely had plenty of opportunities—at school, at family gatherings and weddings, and in business meetings, large and small. And like it or not, there will be plenty of times in your future that you will be called upon to present.

Employers consider presenting an essential skill. Some 35 million Power-Point, Keynote, or other slide deck presentations are said to be given every day. The ability to present effectively matters:

- In a study of four hundred employers, "Oral Communications" was ranked as *the* most important business skill, and considered "Very Important" by more than 95% of those surveyed.
- In a study of company directors, 63% believed that presentation skills are more important for career success than intelligence or financial aptitude. Over one-third of these directors felt that poor presentation skills had hindered their career.
- Warren Buffett told MBA students, "You can improve your value by 50% just by learning communication skills—public speaking."

Even fashionistas agree on the importance of presenting well. *Glamour Magazine* says public speaking is "the #1 work skill you need!"

One's ability to present effectively, or not, is on display, and presentations are great branding opportunities—*if* you do a good job. According to venture capitalist Roger McNamee, "You could do enormous harm to yourself . . . The [presentation] is like a shark. It can't sit still; it either is building or destroying your brand."

Look Out Above!

If you don't like to present (yet), you're not alone. Speaking before a group ranks as people's top anxiety-provoking event, more than fear of heights, flying, spiders, or even death. As Jerry Seinfeld observed, this means most funeral attendees would rather be in the casket than give the eulogy. Studies suggest more than 70% of the adult population fears public speaking. Even Warren Buffett dropped out of his first Dale Carnegie public-speaking course because he was afraid to speak up.

Why the anxiety? Because, we believe, most presenters:

Fear making a fool of themselves. They know that audience members are forming an impression of them and are afraid of being exposed as lacking in this critical business skill.

Don't know how to present. Whatever they learned in high school speech class is long forgotten. Public speaking is usually an elective in college, and most people don't elect it. MBA schools do teach it, but they reach only a small subset of those in business. Surprisingly, few law schools require their students to take a course in public speaking. Once in the business world, it's difficult to learn good technique by watching others because most business presenters are sorry (as we say in the South), especially with graphics. They unwittingly teach what *not* to do.

Don't put in the time. A presentation worth giving takes time to create and learn. Great speakers make their presentations look effortless, but they are anything but. For many, starting is the hardest part, so they delay preparing and run short on time. When the appointed time comes, their presentation isn't ready, and they aren't ready to give it. As a result, they're anxious, and their audience senses their discomfort. Soon their audience is uncomfortable as well!

And so, most business presentations are boring and largely ineffective. Whether the presenter makes a lot of money or enjoys a lofty title provides no assurance he or she knows how to present. Some of the worst offenders are investment bankers and "chief" economists.

To maintain my law license, I must attend Continuing Legal Education (CLE) courses each year. I don't know if practicing law makes one inherently terrible at creating effective slideshows, but the CLE presentations I've suffered through suggest this may be the case. Some of the best sleep I enjoy is in the dimly lit Bar Center auditorium.

The higher you go, the more you will be called upon to speak. Indeed, your ability to present will likely impact how high you go. One Fortune 50 executive sums up what is true in most companies: "Almost no one [attains] an executive position without being an excellent presenter."

To further your career, you *want* opportunities to present. It means you're in the game and visible. Given that most people don't like to present and don't do it well, public speaking provides an opportunity for you to affirm your value and further differentiate yourself. Keep this in mind when you're asked to deliver financial results, discuss how your team can support other teams, or kick off a project. Perfect your skills and you'll further your career not only when you speak within your company, but also when it's your turn to make a sale, raise capital, or speak to those in your industry.

What we offer here will serve you well your entire career, both when flying solo on your own presentations and when providing support to your boss or other colleagues on their presentations. We'll first describe a proven structure that ensures you make your topic clear, provide a roadmap, deliver an audience benefit, and conclude with a call to action. We'll then examine techniques to create effective graphics. Doing that—though not difficult—is rarely achieved. Finally, we will explore delivery techniques—how to learn your presentation and then give it effectively.

Countless people have become accomplished public speakers who started as anything but. If you learn, practice, and consistently apply the techniques that follow, you will become a persuasive presenter.

Over my career I have given countless presentations—to employees, to investors and industry colleagues, and to college and MBA students. I've come to understand the techniques that work. Whether most business presenters know these techniques I can't say; what I can say is that they don't apply them. There's an exciting future for you as a presenter if you do.

PRESENT ROADMAP

Master the Structure

1. Use an Opening Gambit
2. State Your Topic, Objective, and Audience Benefit
3. Preview Your Call to Action
4. Provide a Roadmap and Time Forecast
5. Deliver Your Message
6. Quickly Review
7. End with a Call to Action

Enhance with Graphics

1. Design Your Deck
2. Truncate Text
3. Simplify Data
4. Review and Edit

Stand and Deliver

1. Learn It
2. Give It

Master the Structure

People have been giving presentations since ancient times. What works has long been discovered. Every audience wants to know—and so you must tell them—five things:

- The topic—the reason to meet, the matter to discuss, the issue to be decided
- Your objective—what you intend to accomplish
- Their benefit—why they should care about your presentation
- Your message—what you want them to know
- Your call to action—what the audience could, should, or must do next

By following the seven-step structure that follows, you'll address each of these items. It's your secret sauce—use it in presentations, both small and large, to deliver an audience-focused message.

1. Use an Opening Gambit

Start with an opening gambit. Don't fritter away your one chance to start strong. To launch, take the front of the room (end of the table, podium, stage, whatever), make eye contact with your audience, and pause. Don't

thank some committee or apologize for your nervousness. Don't say "Before I begin," or "I didn't prepare any remarks." Once you say something, you have begun, and the audience expects you to have prepared. If you wish, as you make eye contact, and before you pause, say "Good morning" (or "Good afternoon"). Then begin with your opening gambit.

In diplomacy, an opening gambit is a preliminary or opening tactic. For a presentation, it's your opening remarks. Its purpose is threefold: to give the audience a moment to settle in before you tell them your topic, to capture their attention and interest, and to reinforce—or establish if the audience doesn't know you—your likability. In the quote at the outset of this chapter, Calvin's opening gambit is a story about his trip to the library to explain why he's unprepared.

For small-group company presentations, you're expected to get down to business quickly, so make your opening gambit brief. If presenting the reason why your team missed its numbers, or next year's budget, or the need for a new software platform, it's best not to begin with a story. Begin instead with a thank you for the opportunity to speak and a reference to or humorous quip about something that just happened at the company or externally in the news.

For large-group presentations such as company town halls, training sessions, or a conference, a more extensive opening gambit is required. Opening gambit ideas—all of which you must tie to your topic—include:

- Something in the news that relates to the group you're speaking to
- A question asking for a show of hands, or a rhetorical question to make a point
- A look back in time, or an analogy or familiar saying
- An unusual or shocking fact or statistic
- A personal story

If you can inject humor into your opening gambit, have at it. The humor could, for example, be in how you connect a seemingly unrelated event, fact, or story to your topic.

2. State Your Topic, Objective, and Audience Benefit

Tell them your topic. Your audience must know what it is you're speaking to them about. Transition from your opening gambit to the topic ("which brings us to . . ."). We like a two-part topic sentence: the broad topic followed by the narrower focus of your talk. Such as, "Our topic today is business intelligence software, and, specifically, how we're going to implement our new

platform." Or, "Today we're going to talk about our budget, and how we're going to make our numbers after a disappointing last year."

Tell them your objective. Now that they know what the talk is about, tell your audience what you, the presenter, intend to accomplish. When you're finished with your presentation, what will the audience have gained? Such as, "My objective this morning is to explain what the marketing team can do for you, and how to access our services." Your objective leads to the audience benefit, which comes next.

Tell them why they should care. The audience wants to know, "What does this topic and your objective have to do with me?" Or, to use less genteel phrasing, "Why should I give a damn?" They shouldn't, and won't, unless you tell them why. Help your audience want to hear your presentation by making clear the benefit to them—the What's In It For You ("WIIFY"). Many presenters make no attempt to connect the dots between their message and their audience. Without a message whose primary purpose is to benefit their audience, what the hell are they doing up there? They lose their audience at the start and never get them back.

In the real estate world, conference speakers routinely tell their audience what their company does and how successful it is. Who cares? The burden is on the speaker to make her remarks relevant to me. Tell me how to build my company, or how I can apply what has worked for her, or how I can learn from her mistakes. Tell me something I can use that rewards me for listening.

Don't make your audience try to figure out whether you have anything to say that they should care about. Tell them now—at the outset—the benefit they are about to receive:

- "[Topic] is important to you because . . ."
- "We're discussing [topic] because . . ."
- "You care about [topic] because . . ."
- "[Topic] matters to you because . . ."

The audience benefit could be hearing news you're delivering, following directions you're providing, learning a skill you're teaching, preparing for change with your advice, or using your solution to solve a problem.

Putting your topic, objective, and audience benefit together looks like this:

- Today's topic is marketing and, specifically, implementing new initiatives to attract, close, and retain new customers.
- My objective this morning is for you to learn these initiatives—and the thinking behind them—so that you can effectively implement them.
- Implementing these marketing initiatives is important to you because doing so will defend and increase our market share and ensure the continued financial success of our company.

Topic, objective, audience benefit. Boom, boom, boom. You've now provided an audience benefit that will result once you achieve your objective.

Could you flip the last two items, putting the audience benefit after the topic and before your objective? You could, and doing so should work fine. I prefer ending with the emphasis on the audience—their benefit versus your objective. This order also allows the transition to the audience benefit (e.g. "this is important because") to modify both the topic and your objective.

3. Preview Your Call to Action

Forecast what you want them to do. Business presentations are a call to action. Why give a presentation if no action flows from it? Surely you want people to do *something*, or at least get started along a path. After providing your audience the WIIFY, preview what you'll be asking them to do when you finish. If you don't want to reveal your call to action at the outset of your talk, that's fine, but let the audience know you'll be asking them to act at the end of your presentation. For example, "When I finish, I will ask you to do three things. I will save those until the end."

What do you want them to do?

- If teaching a skill, ask them to use it.
- If providing direction, ask them to follow it.
- If imparting knowledge, ask them to apply it.
- If providing a solution, ask them to implement it.
- If revealing an opportunity, ask them to pursue it.
- If proposing a new product, service, or vendor, ask them to support it.

If you're struggling to find your call to action, keep asking yourself, "To what end?" Why does my audience need to know what I'm telling them? "I just want to keep them informed" isn't good enough. Nor is "I just want to alle-

viate concerns." To what end? Why do they need to be informed? What concerns, and why is it important that you alleviate them? Keep thinking until you find your call to action. Confirm with your manager or whoever directed you to give the presentation that your requested action is the desired one.

4. Provide a Roadmap and Time Forecast

Provide a roadmap. If your presentation is longer than 15 minutes, give your audience a roadmap showing the big-picture organization of your message. Show only the major sections—likely between three and five. A roadmap will make it easier for your audience to understand and retain the information you present.

Forecast the time. When you discuss your roadmap, tell the audience how long you will talk and how long you expect to spend on each major item of your roadmap. By setting audience expectations, you demonstrate your preparation and respect for their time. You'll also alleviate their concern—no doubt a learned response from listening to poor speakers—that you'll speak longer than they expect.

With this introduction you've addressed four of the five questions every audience wants answered. You've stated the topic, your objective, and their benefit, and you've introduced your call to action. If the presentation's length so warrants, you've also provided a roadmap and time forecast. Your audience is relaxed and receptive because it's clear you know what you're doing. It's now time to address their fifth and final question—the message you want them to know.

5. Deliver Your Message

Organize your message using some logical flow. For the body of your presentation, choose a flow structure that makes your message easy to follow. Possible structures include:

Progression

- Flow—steps in a process
- Chronological—events over time
- Numerical—items in an intentional order

Audience-focused

- Problem/Solution—a problem and how we will solve it
- Features/Benefits—what we offer and how it will benefit you

- Opportunity/Realization—an opportunity and how we will capitalize on it

Other

- Parallel—repeat the same structure for each successive item
- Compare/Contrast—how two or more things are alike, or different, or both
- Lyrical song—fact, fact, fact, refrain, then new fact, new fact, new fact, same refrain

Additional structure possibilities include a case study, pilot results, story, and parable. Or a structure you devise. Mix and match flow structures as needed. For example, you could have three major sections, but use a features/benefits or parallel structure approach within them. The test for your organizational plan is whether it's easy for the audience to follow and remember. If your roadmap is easy to follow, your message should be as well.

Make your message interesting and memorable. As you craft your message, liven it up with examples, stories, and analogies. Where possible, make facts and numbers come alive by translating them to images. Doing so will make it easier to understand your message.

> *To illustrate, for example, that a train engineer doesn't feel a thing when a train hits a car, you could point out that a car weighs 3,000 pounds, while the average train weighs 6,000 tons. These are big numbers without context. Instead, you could make them come alive by observing that based on the weight relationship between a train and a car, a train hitting a car is like a car driving over a can of Coke.*

Be as brief as you can while conveying your message. Resist the impulse to tell everything you know. Provide only what your audience needs to know to understand and heed your call to action. The shorter and tighter your presentation, the better.

6. Quickly Review

Briefly restate your best points. If you provided a roadmap, use it as the device for your review. Don't give the talk again! Repeating your roadmap signals to the audience that you're about done. Don't disappoint them.

7. End with a Call to Action

Finish with your call to action. You previewed it earlier or told your audience it would be coming. Now that they've heard your message, ask them to do something with it—what they must, should, or could do next.

Voilà! You now have a presentation structure for your entire career. Learn it and follow it. This structure ensures you address your audience's five key questions. Deviate from it at your peril. Determine what elements of this structure, if any, shouldn't apply to a given presentation and customize it as needed. While every presentation is different, we think you'll be surprised at how little customization is required.

Enhance with Graphics

Once you have written your presentation, consider whether to use graphics —a slide deck—to support your presentation. Not using a slide deck offers these advantages:

- You won't need to prepare a slide deck.
- Your audience can focus on you, and you on them.
- You won't need devices such as a laptop, screen, or remote.
- You won't need a tech guru on site or worry about a tech snafu.
- You can go faster without waiting for your audience to absorb slide content.
- Time spent on graphics can be spent practicing your talk or doing something else.

Slides of any type compete with you for audience attention. As if watching a tennis match, the audience moves from you to your slide, back to you, to your next slide, back to you, *ad infinitum.* The audience must listen to you while reading text or deciphering data. Giving a slide-free presentation is like driving a convertible with the top down and the wind in your hair. Freedom!

If you decide to use graphics, or if you're required to use graphics, then ensure they provide a visual experience that adds to your words. Use your graphics to promote understanding, aid retention, evoke an emotion you want, or add humor. By applying the techniques that follow you'll create uncluttered slides that are quickly "gettable" and that allow more of the audience's attention to be on you.

1. Design Your Deck

Keep your deck design elements simple. You're busy, with lots of demands on your time. The creativity of your slide show is not in your template or your

use of transitions or animations. It's in the content and arrangement of your slides and in your delivery.

Create a consistent look and feel with a simple template. Using a solid, dark background with text in white will make your slides easier for the audience to read and understand. Avoid stock template backgrounds with a wavy blue ocean, clouds, hourglass, scales of justice, seashells, or other nonsense that make your slides difficult to read. Don't use any template that competes with your content.

Check out websites that allow you to inexpensively access professional templates and graphics from illustrators around the world. Current sites include Upwork, 99designs, Fiverr, and DesignCrowd. Even custom work can be inexpensive online.

Make your text stand out. Use one font for the whole deck, size 24-point or larger, with no italics and no underlining (both are hard to read). Choose a simple and readable font that doesn't call attention to itself. Calibri will work fine, as will Futura, Garamond, Gill Sans, Helvetica, Myriad Pro, Rockwell, and others.

Don't distract with transitions. Please, no slides that fly in or out, arrive from top or bottom, or transition side-to-side.

Don't distract with animations. The exception to this would be to use an "appear" animation when you want to progressively reveal text, such as where revealing upcoming items would kill the drama in a top-ten list. But use even this animation sparingly since bullets appearing one by one (on a click) take more time.

Use your roadmap slide to transition between topics. If you provided a roadmap slide as part of your introduction, repeat your roadmap slide when you segue between topics to signal the topic shift and to make your structure more retainable. Highlight the topic that's coming up.

Customize the opening and closing title slides. Use a logo—as appropriate, your company's, or the logo of the company to which you're presenting, or the conference logo—and the name of the event and date.

If you can, creatively illustrate the structure of your message. Consider using designs such as concentric circles, a diagram (cluster, hub-and-spoke, Venn

circles), funnel, matrix, puzzle pieces, organization chart, or pyramid. Again, keep these clear and simple.

2. Truncate Text

Most business presentations have too many text slides and too much text on those slides. Presenters fear freezing with no idea what to say next, so they create slides jam-packed with words—containing much of what they want to say—as a crutch to reduce their anxiety. Audience members seated near the screen can't comprehend all the words in the time the slides appear on the screen. Those sitting in the back and sides of the room don't even try to comprehend the slides.

Limit the number of text slides. Before including a text slide, consider whether you can eliminate or replace it with a slide that has zero words. Consider replacing text with:

- Diagrams
- Graphs
- Maps
- Models
- Photographs
- Site plans
- Sketches
- Videos

Photos that require no text on the slide, and that prompt you to tell a story or make a point, work well.

Limit the amount of text on each slide. The average PowerPoint slide is said to have forty words, and many presenters use slides with far more than forty words.

This Slide Has Forty Words

- As this slide shows
- Forty is too many words
- For your audience to read
- While trying to understand you
- Including words that wrap from one line to another and must
- Be read back-and-forth

The slide has done its job if it reminds you of the point you want to make. It's not there to provide you with the words to express your point. How much text is too much text? Your call, but fewer than forty words. Ideally, limit bulleted text to a few words.

Eliminate word "wraps" in titles and bullets. It's truly bad theater when a slide title is so long that it carries over (wraps) to a second line. Bulleted text shouldn't wrap either.

Eliminate or reduce the number of bullets. Reduce text by reducing the numbers of bullets. As shown above, six bullets are too many. People have given presentations with no bullets and lived to tell the tale. You know what Aristotle would say (think in threes!—see "Write"). Put bullets (if any) in logical order, never randomly, and avoid sub-bullets. If you feel you must have sub-bullets, limit them to one level.

Rather than a slide with three bullets, consider three quick slides with minimal or no words, each akin to an Instagram post with a captivating visual tailored to your point. You want your audience to do the business equivalent of sharing or "retweeting" your ideas.

Avoid quotes and cartoons. Quotes are text and often require dreaded word wraps. If you must use a quote, make it short and pithy. Don't use cartoons. They're rarely funny and the text (including words in balloons) is usually impossible for the audience to read. Having to explain a cartoon makes even a funny cartoon unfunny.

Make each slide pleasing to the eye. Center or otherwise arrange items purposefully, and make bullet spacing proportional up and down the slide. As with your emails, avoid ALL CAPS, as this connotes screaming. Properly size images and get oversized watermarks off your photos!

3. Simplify Data

Similar to text, most business slide decks are overloaded with too much data. Business presenters often lift data slides from other people's presentations, or from strategic plans, annual reports, or other documents. Since the slide makes the desired point and gaining access to the underlying data to recreate the slide is difficult if not impossible, it's tempting to copy the data slide into your slide deck. Unfortunately, chances are the person who created the slide had no clue how to create a proper data slide. If you borrow it, it will now suck the life out of another presentation—yours.

Creating effective data slides means building your data slides from scratch or editing someone else's data slide. Being reasonably facile with PowerPoint, Keynote, or their equivalent is an essential business skill. To create simple and uncluttered data slides:

Have one primary point for each data slide and use the slide title to state it. Not, for example, "Revenue Growth" but "Revenue Growth Increasing."

Show only one chart or graph per slide. Many presenters show two, three, even four graphs on a single slide; multi-graph slides are ineffective—too much data that's too hard to follow.

Use pie charts to show the relationship of individual pieces to a fixed total. Use no more than six slices of data. Combine small items into an "other" category and consider "exploding" or highlighting the most important slice.

Use bar charts to compare quantities (horizontal) or show changes over time (vertical). Use no more than six horizontal or vertical bars. Order the bars logically and consider "exploding" or highlighting the most important bar. Don't put data inside the bars since it's hard for the audience to see.

Use line charts to show trends over time. Use no more than three lines. For clarity, use different colors for each line, and consider making the most important line thicker. To ensure the slide can be understood if printed in black and white, use dashes and dots as well to differentiate lines.

Search and destroy slide clutter. Only the text and data necessary to prove the point of the data slide (as reflected in the title) should be on a slide. On all charts, eliminate unnecessary grid lines, labels, legends, numbers, and text. Round numbers.

Provide (show) attribution. Doing so adds text, but giving credit to your data source is the proper and professional thing to do.

4. Review and Edit

Review your deck, focusing first only on the slide titles. Once you think your slide deck is done, select slide sorter view and go through the deck slide by slide looking at only the titles. Now that you can more easily see your flow, rewrite titles, rearrange slides, and cut unnecessary slides. Once the order and slide titles are what you want, then re-examine every slide. Fix typos and further simplify and unclutter slides by shortening or replacing text or reducing the amount of data.

> *Put your finished slides through the phone test—could a distracted*
> *audience member look up from his phone to glance at your slide, and*
> *immediately grasp the concept? Or the billboard test—could a driver*
> *read and understand them while driving by at 80 miles an hour, while*
> *listening to tunes and eating a McRib sandwich? If so, your slides are*
> *probably OK.*

Ask a colleague to review your deck. For a major presentation, ask a colleague or mentor who excels at presentations to critique (not create) your graphics. As your presentation skills improve, pay it back by helping others in the same way.

> *I taught these techniques to my teams and yet, when asked to review a*
> *slide deck for an upcoming presentation, I saw improvement but still*
> *too much clutter. Old habits die hard, particularly since what we're*
> *advocating here is work. It's work to replace text slides and to reduce*
> *the number of bullets and words in bulleted text. It's also work to create*
> *simple data slides instead of borrowing confusing slides. And it's even*
> *more work to learn the presentation since its content will not be on the*
> *screen to read.*

Pay attention to the graphics the next time you attend a presentation. See if you don't agree that the slides of most presenters are incomprehensible due to distracting templates, too much text, and too much data. Effective slides are the exception, not the rule. On rare occasions you will find presenters who use graphics effectively. You might wonder where they learned to do it, since so few people seem to know. Now you know.

Stand and Deliver

You've created a strong presentation—audience-focused, substantive, and action-inducing. But unless you deliver it effectively, much of its impact will be lost. Sad to say, but an average presentation well delivered has more audience impact than an outstanding presentation poorly delivered. Let's not let that happen to you.

1. Learn It

With or without a slide deck, your focus should be on your audience, not on reading notes or text slides. You must learn your presentation.

Create notes. Learn your talk by creating notes as you practice. Create them in bullet form rather than complete sentences. If using slides, determine for every slide what you want to say. Learn your slide progression to create smooth transitions. During this practice process you'll further cut, edit, and perhaps reorder your slides.

Should you use your notes for the actual presentation? We've all ordered a meal from a waiter or waitress who doesn't write down our order. We don't think, "What a fabulous memory!" We think, "My order's going to be screwed up." We just want them to get our order right, the likelihood of which is increased if they write it down. Likewise, you won't get credit for speaking without notes. Since most business presenters rely on some form of notes, the absence of notes isn't required or expected. Use notes if doing so makes you more comfortable and reduces anxiety, or if you're concerned about forgetting something. It's scary to get up in front of a large group without notes.

I prepare notes and then decide just before speaking whether to use them. They help me learn my talk, and knowing I have them alleviates jitters. And nothing stops me—or you—from bringing notes to the front and not using them.

I try to confine my notes to the front sheet of a stiff-backed legal pad. This prevents me from having to flip through pages or risk dropping them (like golf tees). A stiff-backed legal pad also works better for roaming than do loose sheets of paper or index cards.

But . . . it's nearly impossible to present with energy while reading. A risk of using notes during your presentation is that you'll read too much, especially so if you use notes and a slide deck. As you think about using notes, consider:

- No slides and no notes allow you to focus fully on your audience and them on you.
- Notes and no slides result in some loss of audience focus as you look at your notes.
- Slides and no notes result in some loss of audience focus as you look at your slides.
- Both slides and notes result in more loss of audience focus as you look at notes and screen.

Practice out loud. Say your presentation out loud when you practice, including the transitions between slides. Not "When I get to this slide, I'll say something about the economy." Only by talking out loud will you eventually discover the phrasing and word choices you want. Use base verbs and familiar words. Go easy on modifiers and avoid business buzzwords (see "Write").

As you practice, eliminate garbage phrases that consume time, appear pompous, and add nothing (see "Write"). Try also to eliminate "verbal diarrhea" such as um . . . er . . . you know . . . like . . . uh . . . I mean . . . well . . . and so . . . mmm . . . ah. The mouth is speaking while waiting for the brain to engage. The only known cure for verbal diarrhea is knowing what you want to say and practicing it out loud. Notice where you flounder—that will tell you where you haven't mastered your phrasing, word choice, or transition. Decreasing verbal diarrhea is a sign you're mastering your presentation.

Space your practice. As with your writing, walking away for a while will allow new perspective when you return. Keep practicing from beginning to end without stopping until you can present smoothly.

To hear how smooth you sound, record your verbalization on your phone and play it back. Listen for garbage phrases and verbal diarrhea. Find synonyms for words you struggle to pronounce. For me, for an embarrassingly long time, my Achilles' heel was "segue."

Memorize your launch. Memorize starting with your opening gambit and continuing through your topic, objective, and audience benefit. Doing so is an antidote to anxiety at a time you're most nervous, and allows you to start fully focused on your audience. Don't worry about appearing stilted; you won't say it exactly as you learned it.

Time your presentation. Once you can smoothly deliver your presentation, say it out loud, clicking slide by slide, and time it. Otherwise, you can't accu-

rately forecast its total length or the time you'll spend on each item on your roadmap slide. Only by knowing in advance that your presentation won't run long can you relax—and not rush by speaking fast—as you give it.

I once traveled cross country to San Francisco to speak at a conference. Being an experienced speaker, I thought I could predict the length of my talk without timing it. Guilt got the better of me, so just before bed I gave the talk a timed walk-through in my hotel room. It was twenty minutes too long. I was up half the night cutting slides and learning new transitions. The talk got better as it got shorter, but this late-night fire drill was a self-inflicted injury.

Don't use a rule of thumb to predict the length of your talk based on the number of slides. Some slides, such the humorous ones, are on and off in seconds. Others will appear on the screen for a minute or more while you tell a story or explain data. Every talk is different. Time it and, if needed, shorten it.

Get feedback in rehearsal. All your presentations are important because they reflect on you, but some are more critical than others. For those, try to get feedback during the rehearsal stage. Ask for comments on your content, graphics, and delivery.

Prepare for what might go wrong. Anticipate glitches. What if some aspect of your technology fails, and you must give your presentation without slides? What if the speaker in front of you talks too long and uses your time, thereby forcing you to shorten your presentation? What if she uses some of your best content? Think about what you'll do. Freaking out isn't an option.

During a going-public road show in Europe my co-presenter got laryngitis before our first stop in Amsterdam. He was to give the back half of every presentation. For the first few days of the road show, I had to present both halves and handle all questions. You never know.

Practice until you master your presentation. The best way to overcome pre-presentation nerves is to remind yourself before you begin that you have a message that will benefit your audience, that your graphics enhance this message, and that you're ready to deliver it well.

> *A little fear is probably a good thing as it gets our attention and helps us focus. Some of the most accomplished musicians admit to stage fright before performances. If they're a bit nervous, we're certainly entitled to be.*

2. Give It

All your work is for this moment. It's showtime—time to stand and present with confidence. Take a deep breath, exhale, and get up there.

Connect with your audience. When giving your presentation you have several possible places to look: (1) at your feet, (2) at the ceiling, (3) at your notes, (4) at your slides on the screen or wall, or (5) at your audience. The magic is in looking mostly at your audience. Since your presentation is for and about them, your focus must be on your audience.

The secret is to speak only when making eye contact with your audience. Proper technique when using notes is to briefly look down at your notes, see what you need, then look up and speak. If using slides, try to avoid a set-up where you must turn around and face the screen to see the slide displayed. If you must turn backward to do so, don't talk while looking back. Glance at the slide, turn back to face your audience, and then talk.

To connect, make eye contact with different members of the audience. Look at a face for a few seconds before moving on. See your audience not as an amorphous blob, but as individuals who want to hear what you're saying.

Present with energy. Be alert and alive, engaged, natural. Caring about your topic and your audience, and delivering a message you believe in, should provide energy enough. Words ring true only if consistent with accompanying body language. When your body language and speech conflict, your audience will subliminally believe your body language. Saying "this merger will be a positive for every one of you," in a low voice, without energy, without eye contact, and while slumping over the podium, hardly inspires confidence.

Match your tone to your message. As you progress in your career, you'll be asked to deliver "hard" messages. Sometimes you'll be the presenter of bad news: "The accounting shop is moving from Seattle to Washington, DC," "The company is selling this division," or "There will be no salary increases this year." Or, "The company is being sued into oblivion." Whatever the reality of their situation, people need to know it to adapt and move forward. Be empathetic and deliver tough news with compassion.

Don't hurry. Speak with energy but at a pace your audience can follow. Our normal conversational cadence is often too fast for presentations. You timed your talk and know you'll finish within the expected time, so there's no need to race through it. Talking too fast is often associated with nerves or, worse, deceit. Think of commercials that preclude trust because the offer limitations or drug side effects are spoken so fast as to be incomprehensible.

Be in the moment. Consider what has happened shortly before your presentation and incorporate timely remarks into your talk. These remarks could include world or national events, an event at your company, or something said by a prior speaker. If your presentation is being given in the context of outside events that are on everyone's mind—in other words, an elephant in the room such as a natural disaster, a plummeting stock market, an industry in disruption—address these events if only to acknowledge that your topic pales in comparison.

Being in the moment also means offering spontaneous, perhaps humorous, remarks in response to something that happens during your presentation. If someone ran naked across the stage during your talk, would you say something about it? Here's betting yes. Since a streaker is unlikely to appear, look for something else. The height of the microphone, something an audience member said to you before you started, a comment by another speaker (never be derogatory), something gone wrong.

I once worked with an assistant prone to typos. I suspected a typo lurked in my slides, but I couldn't find one. The presentation seemed perfect. As I began the talk, I found the typo—on the title slide! Since likely some audience members caught the typo while others did not, I pointed it out and made a joke about how I like to set a low bar for my talks by inserting a typo right at the outset. The audience had a laugh at my expense. I was in the moment.

Why be in the moment? Because it makes your presentation feel current, not canned. It creates a bond between you and the audience—your talk is being experienced together.

If at a loss for words, pause. As awkward as it may feel, pausing in silence beats verbal diarrhea. Trust that in the pause your mind will figure out what to say next. It will—if you are prepared. If doing so takes longer than ex-

pected, use "and" to keep your flow going while you wait for your brain to engage. Not perfect, but better than other forms of verbal diarrhea.

> *Recognize that the audience empathizes with you and wants you to succeed, if for no other reason than it's in their best interest. They want the benefit you promised from your presentation. Only a jackass or rival for that next promotion hopes you struggle with your presentation.*

Use humor, if comfortable. Don't worry if humor doesn't come naturally for you, as it's not expected or required for business presentations. If it does, humor is persuasive because it promotes likability. It helps you fit in. Misdirection, surprise, and a self-effacing wit will make your audience at ease and receptive to your message. Ensure your humor is appropriate in all respects, and never embarrass a colleague.

> *I recently served as best man at my brother's wedding and delivered the customary wedding reception speech. Despite some anticipatory dread (hell yeah, I was nervous), the speech must have been OK, as friends, relatives, and other guests gave me props and supplied me with drinks for the rest of the night. Yes, it was an open bar, but the point remains: people told me I did a nice job, and that felt great. Assuming you've prepared, once you get a minute or two into your presentation your anxiety will fade. You'll be rolling, and at that point a presentation can become pretty damn fun.*

End calmly and confidently. Don't race through final slides or announce you didn't say all that you wanted to. Time's up—you're done. Smile, pause, say "thank you," and enjoy any accolades that follow. You provided an audience benefit, as reflected by their appreciation.

Conclusion

You now know how to present in terms of structure, graphics, and delivery. Some presentations will go better than others, especially at first. You're learning, so no matter the outcome, "get back on the horse" and keep giving presentations. Follow the *Look Out Above!* guidance, and presenting will move

from intimidating to rewarding. As you improve, and as you receive increasingly positive feedback, you'll experience less stress and hopefully welcome or even seek out opportunities to speak. Your ability to present will become an important part of what you bring to your organization. You'll know you're becoming exceptional when people look forward to hearing you, and when you become the speaker no one wants to follow.

Application: Panels

Time to venture out into the industry. Your first business speaking foray outside your organization will likely be serving on a panel. Most panels are structured like this:

1. Introduction—The moderator introduces the topic and its significance to the audience, and then introduces the panelists. Sometimes the moderator gives a short presentation before introducing panelists, or each panelist gives a short presentation.
2. Discussion—The moderator asks questions and comments on answers. Panelists respond to questions and react to comments from others. The moderator guides the discussion.
3. Question and Answer (Q&A)—Audience members ask questions. One or two panelists (usually not all) respond to each question. After the panel concludes, the moderator and panelists talk with audience members.

Industry events use the panel format extensively. It requires less advance work for the participants, which is why people agree to be on panels in exchange for corporate and personal exposure. For panelists, there is no presentation to write, no slide deck to prepare (usually), and a moderator is responsible for asking questions and making the event flow. Sounds easy, right?

Wrong. Panels are a trap for those who fail to prepare. You're in front of industry peers, and your reputation (and that of your company) is at risk. Most panels have three or four participants, not counting the moderator. Often one panelist offers mundane comments and comes off as out of his depth. He may be at a lower organizational level than other panelists, or it may only seem that way. Another panelist shines by offering insightful, thought-provoking comments that provide audience value. The contribution of the remaining panelists is fine, but not memorable. How do you avoid being the weak link and, over time, become the star panelist?

Agree to be on the panel only if the topic is in your area of expertise. You're more likely to perform well and to reflect positively on yourself and your company if you're deeply familiar with the subject. If not, you'll spend an inordinate time preparing and still risk exposure as the weak link.

Push for advance calls. A good moderator holds one or more advance calls with panelists to make introductions, devise questions, and decide who will answer which questions. Through this process panelists will know the questions and their order, and which ones will be asked of them. The moderator may try to interject drama by finding panelists who disagree on topics and

will argue different sides. A lazy moderator does none of this—you meet him for the first time at the conference. However challenging, try to mitigate the effects of a lazy moderator by pushing for advance calls. For the good of all, someone must drive the preparation process.

Prepare. Draft your answers in bullet form, prepare notes, and practice out loud. If you like, take your notes with you. Prepare too for Q&A time. What would you ask if you were in the audience? Fair game are questions the moderator asked other panelists but you didn't address. Think of a few of the most likely and difficult questions, and draft talking points in response.

Perform. The key once again is to offer remarks that benefit the audience. Otherwise, why would they care about what you say? Tell them how they can apply what you're saying to their business. Tell them what in your experience works, or what you recommend they try. If the situation calls for it, have the courage to give an opinion and defend it. If your reasons make sense, the worst that will happen is you'll eventually be proved wrong (you'll be fine).

Make it enjoyable for the audience. They're at a conference! They could be returning emails, holding meetings with other attendees, or having an early drink, but they've chosen to listen to your panel. Take it seriously but make it fun. Interject humor into your remarks when appropriate. Tell stories. Use analogies. Make them glad they came.

Consider deflecting questions to other panelists. If asked a question that's not in your area of expertise, or to which you have nothing relevant to say, consider directing it to another panelist. Respond with "that's not my area of expertise," or "someone else may be better suited to answer that." Better to deflect than give a weak answer.

Look interested and be interested. Sit up, sit still, and pay attention when others are speaking. You're still being evaluated by the audience, and you can't comment upon or address remarks you weren't listening to (and your mom's not there to whack you when you fidget).

Disagree agreeably. When you're speaking and the moderator or a panelist interrupts you to disagree, you've still got the floor and can respond calmly and professionally. If, after you've finished on a topic, another panelist says something you disagree with, don't contort your face or shake your head in disapproval. That's disrespectful. Remember the remarks you disagree with and address them if the moderator affords you the opportunity.

Don't promote yourself or your company. Doing so is bad form. Being a lively, effective panelist is promotion enough.

Stay after and talk with audience members. And email your moderator and fellow panelists afterwards to say thanks for a great experience and to wish them continued success. Wait for the phone to ring. In time, you'll be a sought-after panelist. After that, maybe a moderator.

Question and Answer

1. My presentation will involve Q&A. Any thoughts on how to handle?

Decide when to take questions. For external presentations, usually questions come after the conclusion of your presentation. Likely an internal audience will interrupt with questions whether you want them to or not. If you want a lively, informal exchange, tell your audience to feel free to ask questions as you go. Doing so risks interrupting your flow but promotes audience involvement. Decide which approach you think works best.

Don't comment on the question. You're up there to answer questions, not opine on their quality. Don't say, "That's a great question." You may appear to be groveling. And, unless you say that in response to every question, other questioners may feel slighted. "Why didn't she say that about my question. Isn't my question a great question, too?"

> *"That's a great question" is often a reflex response to buy time to think. In law school my constitutional law professor asked difficult, seemingly unanswerable questions. Desperate for something to say, I would respond, "That's a great question." To which he would reply, "I know."*

Spare us "I get that question a lot" or "I'm glad you asked that." If so, why didn't you address it during your remarks? Lose clichés such as "To be perfectly frank" or "To tell you the truth." Aren't you always frank and truthful? Why suggest otherwise? These empty phrases are also used by presenters to buy time to think. If you need time, take a deep breath and pause. Or, if you feel the need to say something, say "Thank you for the question."

Understand the question, answer the question, then stop. Ask for the question to be repeated or restated if you didn't hear or understand it. If your audience is large, repeat the question for the benefit of those who didn't hear it, in your own words if necessary to promote clarity. If the question can be answered by "yes" or "no," start your answer with "yes" or "no." You have now answered the question. Then provide any explanation you feel is needed to provide a complete answer. Once you've answered the question, move on. Don't use the question as a launching pad to address other topics, and don't raise a related question and answer it. The audience has already heard a presentation from you; they don't want another one.

If you don't know the answer to a material question, you may lose the good-will from your presentation by appearing to be a fraud who's been exposed. But if you don't know, you don't know. Say so, and perhaps volunteer to get back to the questioner.

Handle hostile questions appropriately. For external presentations or panels, if the hostile question is in your view inappropriate or one you're not willing to respond to, explain why and keep moving. For internal presentations you get no such option. To deal with a hostile question:

1. Pause a moment to think, while maintaining eye contact with the accuser—if you look away, you may appear to have something to hide.
2. Rephrase the question to remove ugly insinuations and state it politely—"Why are you ripping off the customer?" becomes, instead, "Let me tell you about our pricing."
3. Answer the question as you rephrased it, responding to the audience, not the accuser.

When you answer, don't repeat ugly, accusatory buzzwords. To do so is to "water the weed." People will have then heard the ugly word (the weed) twice and be doubly inclined to believe it. And so: "Why is your company butchering the environment?" Watering the weed: "Butchering the environment? We're not butchering the environment!" Question rephrased: "Let me tell you what my company is doing to protect the environment."

End strong (again!). Signal the end of Q&A by stating you'll take one or two more questions. When you've taken your last question, the last thing you say shouldn't be, "Well, if there are no more questions, I guess we're done." Say something to wrap up positively such as asking the audience to remember your call to action. Then thank them and sit down.

2. I've got to give a speech. Any additional thoughts?

While it's unlikely you'll be giving speeches early in your career, *Look Out Above!* is here to help when your time for speechifying comes. The graphics and delivery techniques already discussed apply in full force when giving a speech. The seven-step presentation structure applies as well with the following nuances:

Meet and greet audience members before you start. Doing so will help reduce your anxiety, and you'll appear in full control.

Control the introduction. The audience experience starts with your introduction. If someone will introduce you, don't hand her your résumé beforehand and hope she parses it to pull out a few key facts to show you're qualified to speak on the topic. To ensure a better introduction, do the parsing yourself and provide bulleted talking points. (Similarly, if you're introducing a speaker, don't read his résumé to the audience. Your job is simply to demonstrate to the audience that the speaker is qualified to speak to the topic. Distill your introduction to a few interesting talking points and stop.)

Extend your opening gambit. It will be longer, more challenging to devise, and more important for a speech than for a small-group company presentation. Since this broader audience doesn't know you, your likability must be established. Your opening gambit must grab the audience's attention and make them receptive to you and your message.

Feigning doubt at the outset about your speaking skill is a rhetorical device known as dubitatio: "I don't do this often, so please bear with me." The concept is to lower expectations and then crush them. Doubt may work fine for non-business talks such as a wedding toast, and maybe for your first few business presentations. After that, likely you'll be expected to present as part of your job. Therefore you might want to retire this ploy from your business repertoire.

We don't recommend telling a joke as your opening gambit. You can't predict its success, and even if it gets a laugh, it's awkward. You're not there to tell jokes.

Remember: Topic, Objective, Audience Benefit. Ensuring that your external presentation adds value to the audience will make you "famous by Friday" in the speaking world. Remember to make clear the WIIFY that you're providing to your audience.

Provide your qualifications if necessary. If there will be no introduction, or if you aren't sure whether someone will introduce you, be prepared to provide your qualifications in a sentence or two. The time to do so is after you've established the audience benefit, and before you provide a roadmap. Consider this transition: "Who am I, to speak to this topic?"

Customize your presentation. Do some homework to understand your audience. Learn what matters to their company, industry, and world, and what is happening now. Refer to this information in your remarks.

As time permits, and if appropriate, involve the audience. Consider the following audience participation devices either as part of your opening gambit or within your talk:

- Ask a rhetorical question.
- Take questions up front, or as you go.
- Ask questions up front, or as you go.
- Conduct a demonstration with an audience member.

Don't overdo the audience participation—you've got an objective to accomplish and an audience benefit to deliver in a limited time. Involve your audience too much, and you risk losing control of your presentation. Make any audience involvement relevant and anticipate how it might backfire.

Create a closing device. For a speech to finish strong, you need something to provide a sense of closure. Tie back to your opening gambit or end with a brief story. Consider an emotional appeal to send out a crowd fired up about your call to action.

3. Any final presenting tips and tricks?

Adopt the mindset that your presentation is for and about your audience. It's about the audience accessing the benefit you promise and heeding your call to action. Focusing on delivering a beneficial message will result in a better presentation and may reduce your anxiety.

Get familiar with the room and test the tech. The first time you hear yourself deliver the presentation shouldn't be when you give it. If possible, practice in the room where you'll be presenting. Stand up front, look out at the room, and imagine the seats full. Click through your slides, if using slides, and speak out loud as you go.

Test everything! Technical errors I've experienced include flash drives that won't load, videos that won't play, videos that play but with no audio, dead batteries in the projector, clickers that can't be found or don't work, and the inability to access the internet or obtain adequate signal strength.

Don't carry a visible ream of paper to the podium. The audience will see it and, anticipating a long-winded presentation, dislike you before you've said a word.

Make sure your audience can hear you. Otherwise, it's impossible for you to be effective. If you have a microphone, let it do the work. Don't shout—no audience likes to be screamed at or talked to loudly. Some "experts" teach to start softly and then turn up the volume. Others teach to start loud, then turn down the volume, so people must move to the edge of their seat to hear you. Don't play such games. If people can hear you, and you're speaking with energy, your volume will go up and down naturally . . . and you'll do fine.

Make sure your audience can see you and your slides. If you dim all the lights, the audience will focus on your slides instead of you, or fall asleep, or both. If the room is bright, the audience may have a hard time seeing your slides. If possible, keep the lights on and dim only the lights above the screen, while you stand out in the light.

Stand in one place, or roam as you prefer and as the venue permits. Do whatever is most comfortable for you. Try removing any barriers between you and the audience such as a podium or table. Stand in one place or walk as you talk; either works fine. If you are using a slide deck, stand mostly on the left side of the screen (from the audience's perspective), so the audience will return their eyes to you in anticipation of reading the next slide from left to right. If you roam and are using a slide deck, try not to block the screen as you move about.

Don't let your hand movements distract from your message. Some hand movements present an unpleasant picture: hands lowered in front of the body covering the crotch ("male fig leaf"), arms crossed covering the chest ("female fig leaf"), arms lowered, one hand clasping the other hand behind the back ("commander"), one arm hanging limp with the other arm crossing the body and holding the limp arm ("wounded soldier"). Putting your hand in a pants pocket may appear too casual and, if that hand rattles keys, jingles change, or fidgets, you may divert attention from what you're saying to what you're doing.

What should you do with your arms? Try letting your arms hang naturally at your side. Bend your elbows. Clasp your hands if you want. Gesture appropriately to what you are saying. "This is a huge opportunity!" . . . "I'm only asking for a small fee" . . . "I try to leave the family, and they pull me back in!"

Don't take someone else's time. You'll be fuming when it happens to you—the prior speaker prattles on and forces you to shrink your talk (the one with an actual audience benefit) in real time as you give it. Running long is bad enough—taking someone else's time is inexcusable.

Consider these action steps. From easier to more challenging:

- Observe closely and learn from good (few) and bad (many) speakers.
- Ask a question when attending presentations—think of something!
- Speak to civic organizations and groups at schools, community colleges, churches.
- Volunteer to give a presentation at work and solicit feedback.
- Take a public speaking class.
- Teach a class.

Pitch!

CHAPTER FOUR

"You don't make progress by standing on the sidelines, whimpering and complaining. You make progress by implementing ideas."

SHIRLEY CHISHOLM, CONGRESSWOMAN, EDUCATOR, AUTHOR

Pitch

We've seen that writing and presenting are top-ranked business skills. Now we'll build on these skills to explore a certain kind of pitch: the pitch of a new idea, for, as Plato says, "Ideas are the source of all things."

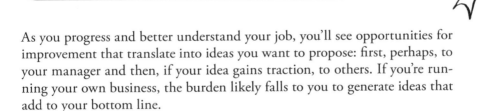

Socrates concurs: "Strong minds discuss ideas, average minds discuss events, weak minds discuss people." Perhaps this explains why Socrates was only occasionally spotted at the check-out counter thumbing through People *magazine.*

4

As you progress and better understand your job, you'll see opportunities for improvement that translate into ideas you want to propose: first, perhaps, to your manager and then, if your idea gains traction, to others. If you're running your own business, the burden likely falls to you to generate ideas that add to your bottom line.

For those ideas to become reality, you must sell them. "But I'm not a salesperson," you may protest. Officially, the Department of Labor says you're in "sales" if you earn your living "convincing others to purchase a product or service." But you're also in sales if you seek to shape decisions or propose new ways of doing things. You're engaged in "non-sales selling," which doesn't involve selling in the statistical sense, but involves convincing colleagues and third parties to agree with and act on your point of view. How could you be a difference-maker otherwise?

This ability to move others to action through non-sales selling is an essential business skill. Author Daniel Pink surveyed more than seven thousand adult full-time workers across a range of professions and asked them how they spent their time, including time spent attending meetings, reading and responding to emails, and having face-to-face conversations. Two major findings emerged, as reported in his book *To Sell Is Human*:

1. People spend 40% of their time at work engaged in non-sales selling.
2. People thought they should be spending even more time doing so.

The respondents considered non-sales selling so essential to their success that—despite spending twenty-four minutes of every working hour engaged in it—they felt they should be doing more of it.

These findings are echoed by the CEO of a leading sales training firm who says, "Our biggest audience now is not professional salespeople, but other kinds of businesspeople who want to get attention for their ideas without seeming pushy."

Some time back late author Tom Wolfe defended the value of a liberal arts education on National Public Radio. He maintained that those who can effectively speak, write, and persuade will ultimately prevail in position and compensation. Wolfe noted that in Roman society, slaves were permitted to take science and mathematics courses, but prohibited from taking rhetoric. The Roman ruling class feared what slaves could do if armed with the power to persuade. Knowing how to persuade is just as powerful today as it was then. You *are* a salesperson. The sooner you accept generating and pitching ideas as an important part of your job, the better for your future success.

The ADP Small Business Guidebook lists as suggested interview questions, "What new ideas or suggestions have you come up with at work?" and "Give me an example of when your ideas were strongly opposed by a co-worker or supervisor. What was the situation? What was your reaction? What was the result?"

Having an idea and pitching it effectively are different things. You'll have only so many ideas and fewer chances to present them. A company can absorb only so much change while executing its business, which limits your opportunities to propose ideas. To make the most of your opportunities, you need to know how to pitch.

You may pitch your own idea or, perhaps more likely at first, you may be asked to work up an idea of your manager or be part of a team that proposes an idea. This chapter is written as if you are proposing your own idea, but its teachings apply equally when you're helping your manager or team analyze an idea, develop the argument, and prepare the presentation. The objective is to succeed—regardless of the source of the idea—with any pitch in which you're involved.

If you follow the *Look Out Above!* process, you'll make the most of your opportunities, raise your profile, and enhance your reputation regardless of outcome. Let's make your ability to sell your ideas, projects, and proposals—and ultimately yourself—another differentiator for you.

PITCH ROADMAP

Prepare
1. Master the Idea
2. Know the Numbers
3. Consider the People
4. Make the Call

Sell
1. Pick Your Spot
2. Set the Table
3. Prove Your Case

Close
1. Listen
2. Respond
3. Call the Question

Prepare

Pitching starts with an idea—one that if implemented could make a meaningful difference at your company. Perhaps by:

- Generating revenue from new products or services, increasing revenue from an existing source, or charging for something now provided for free
- Reducing expenses by improving efficiency or automating processes now performed manually, or eliminating products, services, or reports
- Improving the customer experience, perhaps even if it costs more

- Solving problems that impair effectiveness and cause delays
- Introducing a new tool, or upgrading or switching technology platforms
- Reducing risk, ensuring compliance, or preserving reputation
- Devising a better way to gather and analyze data
- Improving the quality of life at your company

Others have come before you with good and not-so-good ideas. You can't do much worse than the Kool Kardashian Kard, PawPals, or XFL Football. Or the McRib Sandwich, which somehow persists to this day. Somebody pitched—and somebody approved—each one. If you haven't heard of these failures, Google 'em. They're real.

Always be looking for ideas about new products or services, and for ways to do things better, faster, and cheaper. Try to think differently from others— perhaps more steps ahead, or more deeply. When it comes, the idea may take the form of a word, a phrase, a sentence, an image. While ideas come to people in different ways, here are a few ways to get the process going:

- Start with sound subject matter knowledge.
- Identify a problem you would like to solve and give yourself time to think on it.
- Know when you do your best creative thinking and try to arrange your schedule so that at such times you're relaxed and uninterrupted.
- Be ready when inspiration strikes and write the idea down in as much detail as possible.

We can't control how or when a great idea pops into our consciousness. What we can control, to some extent, is the ability to create circumstances conducive to triggering ideas.

Once you have an idea, and before you pitch, you must master the idea, know the numbers, and consider the people.

1. Master the Idea

Be the expert about your idea. As its sponsor, you must be the subject-matter expert who understands every facet of your idea. As the saying goes, "The best way to sound like you know what you're talking about is to know what you're talking about." Only by understanding every aspect can you make an informed decision about whether the idea will work and whether you can

defend it. It's no fun to discover that someone in the room understands your idea better than you, especially if they don't support it.

Why the idea? Why does the company need to act? Is there an important opportunity to be realized or problem to be solved? Does the idea make or save money and thereby increase profit? Does the idea defend current revenue or market share? Does the idea fit with company strategy or a current initiative? Is it consistent with your company's values? Is the idea pioneering in some respect?

What is the idea? What, exactly, are you proposing? How does or will it work? Does it relate to products and services, platforms, or people? Or something else?

What is the do-ability of the idea? Is it possible to execute the idea at a reasonable cost and within a reasonable time? If third-party approvals are required, how likely are they, and how much time and expense will they require? What are the risks, and how can you mitigate them? What are the risks of not acting? What are the opportunity costs, and possible unintended consequences? Assuming the idea is doable, if it's executed as you propose, will it deliver the benefits you envision?

What resources are required? Will the idea pull resources or otherwise impact the daily execution of the business? What will be its ramification on people and teams? How will it affect other initiatives and platforms? Will third parties be involved or affected?

When should the idea be implemented? What is your proposed timing? How long will implementation take? Should the timeline include a pilot or beta test on a smaller scale? Does the timing of your idea need to coordinate with the timing of some other initiative, either in process or proposed? Should the implementation occur in phases?

> *Steve Miller, who ran the Biltmore Estate in Asheville for many years, has a mantra for business success: "Start small, learn, and grow." It's a good approach for pitching and implementing any new initiative, product, or company.*

Make sure you can clearly explain your idea. Even people who want to support you may not be able to do so because they don't understand your idea, particularly if it's technology-related and they don't understand the tech.

> *Use Einstein's test for ensuring you have mastered your idea: "If you can't explain it to a six-year-old, you don't understand it yourself."*

2. Know the Numbers

Calculate and provide investment metrics. Doing so allows the decision-maker to compare the financial impact of competing ideas. Consider where the money to fund the idea can be found, and when it will be needed.

What is the financial potential of the idea? Given the dollar value of the idea versus all costs, what is the projected profit or cost saving? What is the initial-year or start-up cost? What is the annualized cost after the first year ("run-rate" cost)? What other ancillary costs are triggered by the idea, including, if applicable, marketing, maintenance, and training costs? Who pays the costs, and who receives the benefit?

What is the Return on Investment (ROI)? What is the payback period, and is it reasonable? Do you propose other metrics to determine whether the idea is compelling or, if implemented, is meeting projections? If you cannot provide an ROI number, acknowledge it and explain why—and make your best case without an ROI. Some ideas are incapable of being reduced to an ROI number, including ideas necessary to remain competitive.

What are the budget implications of the idea? Where is the money coming from? What impact will your idea have on the budget, both this year and in subsequent years? Are you asking for dollars already in the budget, or do you seek to proceed this year with unbudgeted dollars? Are you asking for dollars for the next fiscal year, ahead of preparation of next year's budget?

When are the payments due? Is the cost to be paid in one lump sum, or in installments over time? What is the timing of revenue generated versus the incurring of costs? An idea that saves money from the get-go is usually welcome any time of the fiscal year. Timing matters if funds need to be found or repurposed.

Expect your numbers to be challenged, so be prepared to defend them.

3. Consider the People

Know the players and what they respond to. When considering the personalities, assess how they are likely to react and what you can do to secure their support.

Decision-makers. Who must approve the idea? What do they value? How do they think? What objections will they raise? Is there agreement on the underlying facts?

Affected teams and people. Whose support within the company do you need? Do you have it, or can you get it? Should you align with someone to pitch the idea? Who, if anyone, will oppose the idea? It's unlikely everyone will be supportive. No matter—if you believe in the idea, push forward and deal with the naysayers.

You (and your team). Consider the trade-offs to you and your team if the idea is accepted. Are you fully committed to the idea? Is the team that must implement it committed? If your idea is approved, are you willing to forgo other team initiatives and projects if necessary?

> *You likely won't be able to answer all these questions. That doesn't mean you shouldn't pitch your idea. By considering these questions before pitching, you'll be better prepared and won't be caught flat-footed.*

4. Make the Call

Through the process of analyzing your idea, you'll refine and improve it. As your idea evolves, consider creating a written "elevator pitch" that expresses the idea in a few sentences. Revisit and clarify this statement as your preparation continues. It will be helpful as people ask you for a brief statement of what your idea is about. Hopefully hearing the elevator pitch will cause them to engage, and to want to know more.

As you have conversations with colleagues, be open to challenges to the idea, especially from people who have your best interests at heart. They may know more than you or see something you don't. And they are likely giving you a preview of challenges to come, which gives you a head start on how to address them. Be grateful rather than defensive—listen and learn.

After analyzing the idea and receiving input, do you still believe in it? Can you pitch it with enthusiasm? Are you willing to put your reputation on the line? Pitching a flawed idea that you should have vetted more carefully may not only waste other people's time but damage your credibility and ability to pitch again. Time to decide: go or no go with your idea pitch.

Sell

1. Pick your Spot

Make your pitch when your proposal has the greatest chance of approval. The Greeks called it *kairos*: an opportune moment when conditions are ideal to persuade. To show that the persuasive moment is fleeting, the Greek god Kairos is depicted with one lock of hair in the front—to grab hold of the opportunity—and bald in the back.

Bad timing can lay waste to a lot of work. At a conference I attended, a comedian told jokes as lunch was being served to five hundred people. Few could hear him over the clanking of silverware and din of conversation, and fewer still paid attention. Predictably, he bombed. Similarly, I was asked to offer "reflections" at one of my high school reunions. No one wanted reflections; they wanted to visit with people they hadn't seen in years. Both the comedian and I failed the moment we agreed to perform under unfavorable conditions. At least the comedian got paid.

To the extent you can, set yourself up for success:

Respect the decision-maker's preferred process for receiving information. Many decision-makers want written materials provided in advance. If doing so is requested or required, you have no choice. While you may wish to control every aspect of your presentation—and don't want the matter decided against you before you've been heard—providing materials beforehand will save pitch time and perhaps result in a decision at the meeting.

Ensure the decision-maker will be present. Idea pitches should be face to face, not via phone or email. Seek to secure adequate time. Ask for more time than you'll need so that you don't run over, rush, or not finish.

Ensure people who support your idea, and people who oppose your idea, will be present. You want both camps there—supporters to advocate for you and opponents to object so you can rebut their concerns with the decision-maker present. Better that than having opponents back-channel their negativity.

Consider the timing. Are things going on at the company that make this a good time to pitch your idea? How is your company performing financially? Is it hitting projections? If it's a publicly held company, are people feeling good about the stock price? What are the company's prospects? Is it growing? If you don't know, ask around. If people are hiding in bathroom stalls to avoid being found for staff cuts, your costly new initiative is unlikely to be well-received.

> *On the other hand, if your company is struggling, maybe your idea is just what it needs. Sometimes you've just got to make your move and say, "What the . . ."*

2. Set the Table

Start with your topic, objective, and audience benefit. Use the presentation techniques discussed. An idea pitch is usually a small-group company presentation. Apply the structure, graphics, and delivery presentation techniques discussed earlier (see "Present"). And so, when making your pitch, after a brief opening gambit, proceed to address:

- The topic—the reason to meet, the matter to discuss, the issue to be decided
- Your objective—what you intend to accomplish
- The audience benefit—why they should care about your presentation

For an idea pitch, add a twist to your statement of objective by making it in three parts:

- Shared viewpoint—shared belief, goal, value, or reality
- Need—the opportunity you seek to realize or the problem you seek to solve
- Solution—your recommendation

To gain agreement from the decision-maker at the start, begin your statement of objective with a viewpoint that you and the decision-maker hold in common. In rhetoric, shared viewpoints are called "commonplaces." A commonplace starts your pitch with empathy since it reflects the decision-

maker's worldview. Identity possible commonplaces that could support your idea:

- Belief—such as the importance of customer satisfaction
- Goal—such as achieving budget
- Reality—such as the difficulty of finding good buys in a crowded market
- Value—such as the importance of defending the company's intellectual property

To pitch a customer satisfaction survey, your set-up—topic, objective, and audience benefit—could look like this:

Topic: Our topic today is measuring customer satisfaction, and, specifically, whether to implement a customer satisfaction survey.

Objective in three parts: As we all know, every dollar of revenue originates from our customers (shared viewpoint). Yet we have no metric to gauge the effectiveness of our customer service and to compare our service to that of our competitors (need). I recommend that we retain XYZ company to work with us to create and implement an annual customer satisfaction survey, and to benchmark our service against competitors (solution).

Audience benefit: An annual customer satisfaction survey will give us the metrics we need to better understand, improve, and sell our service ethic.

Finish your set-up. Your recommendation serves as your call to action. As before, if your pitch presentation will run more than fifteen minutes, provide a roadmap and forecast the time. Refer to your roadmap as you transition between major items. Your set-up is now complete.

3. Prove Your Case

Hopefully, following your set-up, you'll be allowed to proceed. If so, it's time for your argument, rhetorically speaking, where you prove your case and sell your recommendation.

Be selective. Argue only those points necessary to persuade the decision-maker to support your idea. If you insert extraneous matters into your argument, the decision-maker may think she must agree with you on these items as well. Once you've addressed the points that matter, stop.

Choose a flow structure. For an idea pitch, a three-part flow structure could work like this:

1. The opportunity or problem—relevant facts in logical order
2. Your idea—including proof the idea is doable given available resources
3. The benefit if adopted—how things will be better once the idea is implemented

Provide supporting data. Try to prove your idea with data from reliable, unbiased sources, with meaningful sample sizes. Internal data could come from a company pilot, beta test, or case study. External data could come from industry peers who have done what you advocate, and from sources outside your industry that are applicable to your industry. Offer internal testimonials and references from department heads and other key executives, and external ones from peers and experts.

Lawyers have a saying: if the law is on your side, argue the law; if the law is against you, but fairness is on your side, argue the equities; if neither is on your side, throw yourself on the mercy of the court. Here, if your data is meager, but supported by common sense, try overwhelming and irrefutable logic.

Anticipate objections. As part of your preparation, you considered likely objections to your proposal. Have an answer ready for each objection. Beware of casually dismissing objections as unfounded or unlikely—they may be valid, and doing so will almost certainly offend those who raise them. You may have to concede that an objection is valid but argue that your idea is still worthwhile and should be implemented.

Rebut alternatives. Regardless of what others say, you may decide to raise alternatives to your idea—including the status quo—and rebut them to prove your idea is superior. If so, be quick about it. Argue more the strength of your idea rather than the weaknesses of alternative ones.

Politicians use "straw dogs"—softball questions they raise and then knock down. They misrepresent their opponent's position, and don't address the real arguments against their view. The only alternatives suggested by these politicians are obviously flawed. Raising and then shooting down straw dogs is a risky strategy for you, as a sharp decision-maker will see through it.

Offer or accept modifications. You may decide to offer—or to accept—modifications to your idea if you can do so without compromising its effectiveness. Being flexible and conciliatory by incorporating suggestions may help you gather critical support. If you offer alternatives as you present, recognize the risk that people will focus on something they don't like about each option (in which event you'll wish you had just pitched your best option).

Borrow rhetorical techniques as needed. The art of argument is all around you. Learn from argument techniques you observe in the real world. Here are some that may help you with a particular pitch:

Advocate a middle course. Aristotle taught that people prefer a decision that lies between extremes. Perhaps offer multiple options to steer the decision-maker to select your middle option. You could show a continuum that frames the extreme choices and show where your idea lies along that continuum. You likely won't recommend one of the extreme ends, but establishing the ends may help you and others see where various alternatives stand in relation to each another and to the extremes. If your proposal *is* extreme, then acknowledge it and explain why the opportunity or problem demands extreme action.

Appeal to emotion. Emotion trumps logic for getting people to act. But be careful here. Most business leaders respond better to logic than emotion. If overdone, an emotional appeal may be considered unprofessional. For this technique to work, you must genuinely feel the emotion you're seeking to evoke. Your chances for success are better if you're appealing to large groups, and if the appeal comes just before you release your audience. To get your audience to act, you could use emotion to invoke:

- Anger—your competitor is belittling you or playing dirty.
- Commitment—things will be better if your idea is implemented.
- Fear—dire consequences may occur if your idea is not implemented.
- Excitement—there's money to be made for the company and for those listening.
- Pride—your idea will help maintain the company's reputation or leadership position.

Once when I notified a non-performing insurance vendor that we were pulling our account, he started crying. Between sobs, he argued that the loss of our business would have a devastating impact on his earnings and his family's well-being. While I felt terrible (his argument was an appeal to emotion), he put his interests first, and not my company's, and hence was unpersuasive. I had a duty to put my company and our people first, not his needs.

Argue against self-interest. Consistent with "company first," you've come to your recommendation reluctantly due to the weight of the arguments for it or despite the sacrifice it requires of you. Your recommendation is not primarily about you, your department, or your team. It's about what's best for the company.

Argue proven success. Since your idea has worked before or is working now, for us or someone else, it will work again.

Change the discussion to future tense. Past-tense discussions focus on blame—who did it, or who was responsible? Future tense discussions focus on choices—what are the options, and which one is best? Recognize when a discussion is occurring in the past tense and move it to the future tense.

Paint a word picture. Describe a new, better company once your idea is implemented and the opportunity is realized or the problem is solved. Or paint a word picture of what will happen if your idea is not implemented.

Show practical wisdom. Where applicable, sell your experience and common sense. Answer complex questions with "that depends." Don't generalize and provide simple but inadequate answers. The discussion that follows your "that depends" may allow you to clarify the issues and demonstrate your command of the subject matter.

Speak in the language of your audience. Marketing, IT, HR, and other departments have their own lingo. Unless you define them, avoid buzzwords and acronyms that are second-nature to you, but not to the decision-maker. And choose your words carefully. The right words can propel your pitch, while the wrong ones may derail it. If fair, characterize the cost as an "investment" rather than an "overhead expense."

> *When I was coaching MBA students prior to their calling alums to raise money for the student-run real estate fund, one student used the word "contribution." No—the students were asking for an "investment." Notice how that word choice makes both the students' ask—and the alums' decision—easier.*

Avoid killer mistakes. Making these mistakes may damage your credibility and sink your pitch.

Arguing the unarguable. This term refers to making an argument you cannot win—perhaps because it violates a decision-maker's commonplace. For example, if your idea will generate revenue but is in murky waters ethically ("everybody does this"), you'll lose against a decision-maker whose priority is safeguarding the company's reputation. By pitching such an idea, you've set up a fundamental conflict of values. You have no chance of prevailing.

Assuming too much. The "assumptive close" assumes without asking acceptance of the underlying proposal or premise. The life insurance salesperson doesn't ask if you want to meet, but instead assumes you do by asking, "Would you rather meet Monday night at 7:00 or Tuesday morning for breakfast?" If the fallacy of your assumptive close is transparent, your decision-maker could be offended—or laugh at you and your obvious tactic. To be respectful say, for example, "*if* my proposal is implemented" and not "*when* my proposal is implemented."

> *When renting a self-storage unit I was asked, "Would you prefer the platinum insurance option, or the gold option?" Neither! I'm already unhappy about renting a storage unit, and I certainly won't be paying extra for insurance. More benign is ordering a sandwich at the Wendy's drive-thru and being asked whether I want the large fries or the regular-sized fries. I didn't order fries! But since you asked, and I'm hungry, let's go with the large.*

Over-promising or understating obstacles, time, cost, risks. Be objective about the realities of your idea and how its implementation will impact the organization. Tone it down if you hear yourself saying things like "no-brainer" or "slam dunk." Disclosure enhances your credibility and helps ensure that any decision is an informed decision. A decision made without information you failed to disclose is a ticking time bomb.

End strong. In both civil and criminal trials, the party with the burden of proof gets to go first *and* last. It's advantageous to argue last since what's said last—especially if it's a powerful idea—is remembered best. End with a recap of your strongest points so that whatever you say resonates with the decision-maker.

Close

You may win your pitch in one of two ways: (1) your idea is accepted in some recognizable permutation of what you proposed, and/or (2) you leave the

field better off for having proposed it. You're not the decision-maker, so the first item is outside your control. The second item is not. Let's finish the pitch process and try to close the sale.

1. Listen

Hear questions and concerns. You may have been able to present your idea without stopping. It's more likely that once you began, you were peppered with questions that you answered as you went. Sometimes your time allotment will be consumed by answering questions, especially if you provided materials in advance. Regard questions as a positive. They reveal what people are thinking and where they need help to support your idea. People in the room are going to want to be heard and—at least in their view—add value.

Be in the moment and listen. If you trust that you will effectively reply to whatever is said, then you don't need to be distracted by worrying about what to say next. So listen up good, as Mom would say. To do so:

- Stop talking.
- Give the speaker your full attention.
- Interrupt only to ask questions when you don't understand.
- When appropriate, paraphrase important points to confirm your understanding.

But go easy on the cocked head and over-bobbing, as if you've just come back from a $99.95 "Empathetic Listening" seminar.

Attorneys must object to questions posed by opposing counsel during the second or two before the witness answers. If the attorney doesn't, she loses the right to object to the question—and the answer—on appeal. Attorneys who let their mind wander and allow an objectionable question to be answered to their client's detriment will soon be talking to their malpractice carrier. Let this be the level of intensity with which you listen as you respond to challenges to your idea.

2. Respond

Respond to those with opposing arguments in three ways: challenge their facts, challenge their conclusions, and show how your idea is better. As you do, make eye contact when you reply. Studies show that one of the strongest signs of intelligence is looking at those to whom you are speaking during

conversations. We can't all be intelligent, but we can all look intelligent by making eye contact.

Challenge facts. The decision-maker needs accurate facts to make sound decisions. Without agreement on the facts, the decision-maker can't effectively address what to do about them. Listen for and challenge:

Inaccurate "facts." Don't hesitate to respectfully challenge someone's purported facts. False statements of fact offered to rebut your idea must be challenged or resulting decisions may be flawed. If upon challenge the facts prove true, so be it. Gaining agreement on relevant facts—no matter who put them out there—serves the decision-making process.

> *A mentor taught me not to debate what the facts are, but to debate what the facts mean. If, however, you proceed despite disagreement over material facts, you risk adjournment (or worse) to gather facts that people agree on. To ensure agreement among all participants, confirm the supporting facts before you pitch.*

Assumptions, beliefs, or opinions asserted as fact. Point out politely that what is offered isn't a fact. Listen for generalities, since assumptions, beliefs, and opinions often masquerade in this form.

Irrelevant facts. Some facts may be true, or assumed to be true for purposes of argument, but they don't prove the proffered conclusion. Resist a snarky retort like "So what?" to facts like these. A more polite response would be, "That might be true, but I don't think it pertains here."

Statistics and "expert opinion" offered against your position. Put statistics offered against your idea through the same filters you applied when choosing your own statistics. Are they from reliable, unbiased sources, and with meaningful sample sizes?

Challenge conclusions. Question a conclusion when you don't dispute the facts but disagree that they lead to or require the conclusion asserted against you. For example, we can agree that winters seem to be getting colder here in North Carolina, but that doesn't disprove global warming worldwide. The facts relevant to your idea pitch may equally or better support another conclusion—like yours.

Show your idea to be better. Accept the opposition's facts and conclusion but argue that your proposal is better at realizing the opportunity or solving the problem. Some solutions (yours) are better than others. "Let's agree for purposes of discussion what you say is correct, but . . ." Or, "What you say is true, but . . ." If you accept someone's facts and conclusion, say so! Accepting the other side's facts—and agreeing with their conclusion—may help sell your idea. Not only are you being fair, but you've crystalized competing proposals for the decision-maker. The issue for the decision-maker is now framed—whose solution is best?

If someone asks you a question and you don't know the answer, say so. Not ideal, but better than undermining trust by saying something that reveals you don't know the answer and are trying to hide it. If the question—and information the question solicits—has little relevance to your idea, point this out to prevent irrelevant questions from derailing the success of your pitch. If the question is relevant, beware trying to minimize its importance. You may need to offer to go get more pertinent information.

3. Call the Question

Ask for approval. At some point you must ask that your idea be approved, either as you proposed it, or as modified after discussion. Perhaps when you sense the tide is turning in your favor, or when the discussion seems talked-out.

> *There are times in every pitch when silence on your part is called for to allow—or to force—others to talk. When you've called the question, let the silence hang and don't speak until you get a reply. If the decision-maker says "Yes," stop selling!*

If your proposal is accepted, address next steps. The idea must now be implemented, which likely means extra work for you and your team. Honor the commitment—stated or implied—that you've made. The need to sell your idea doesn't stop with the decision-maker or with approval; you must "sell after the sale" to those throughout the company whose support is required for implementation.

Look Out Above!

If the idea is received enthusiastically, don't be shocked if naysayers suddenly become supportive or even claim to have originated it. Or, if the idea goes down in flames, others may say they told you so or disavow any prior support of it. No matter. Such is human nature.

It's possible that a decision will be tabled. The decision-maker may require more facts, or time to consult with someone, or to think on it. People have their own styles, as you'll quickly learn. Action-biased types will want no more meetings—and a decision now. Professor types tend to move at a glacial pace and want more meetings—and may never make the decision.

If your proposal is not accepted, accept the outcome gracefully. No matter how strongly you believe in your idea and how well you sell it, the answer may still be no, or not now. You accepted the risk that your idea might be rejected the moment you decided to proceed with the pitch. Defeat can be tough to take because of your investment in the idea. Rejection isn't fatal, and may not even be final if you choose to revive the idea at a more propitious time. But not all ideas will resonate, and you don't know everything going on at the company that affected the decision. Yours could be a fine idea but not be approved due to lack of funds, inopportune timing, or competing initiatives deemed more compelling. Or the decision-maker may simply see the world differently.

If your proposal doesn't carry the day, thank the decision-maker for the opportunity to present the idea and for her time and consideration. Make sure all concerned know that you accept and will support the decision, and remain committed to the company.

See the pitch process as a learning opportunity. Rejection of your idea isn't a rejection of you. While you don't want to amass a track record of unsuccessful pitches, likely you're better off for having properly prepared and pitched the idea. You'll have shown initiative, acquired insight into how the approval process works at your company, and gained exposure to senior management. The experience you've gained will serve you well over time. Your idea is still on record, and your initiative and willingness to risk will be noticed.

Document your lessons learned. Regardless of outcome, and while the details are still fresh, put in writing your lessons learned. Jot down what went well, and what you'll do differently next time. Include questions you were asked that you didn't anticipate. You've gained valuable experience; take the time and make the effort to make the most of it.

Conclusion

You now know how to analyze and pitch an idea. That puts you ahead of the class, and ready to pitch an idea effectively when the occasion arises.

Lawyers talk about three closing arguments they give to end every trial: the one they planned to give, the one they gave that the jury heard, and the better one they thought of afterwards on the drive home. You won't give your pitch precisely as planned. You'll adjust to the realities of the moment, including the questioning by decision-makers. And, like anyone who has pitched an idea or proposal, after you're done you'll see an argument you missed, or a better way to articulate an argument you made. It's a process. Once you've pitched a big idea, either internally at your company or externally to outsiders, you're in the game. If you follow the *Look Out Above!* guidance, your technique will improve with every idea you pitch.

Application: External Pitches

Rather than an internal pitch at your organization, here your idea pitch is external. You're pitching to a third party to buy your product or retain your services, or invest in your company, or loan your company money (or hire you if you're back in the market). Everything said about preparing, selling, and closing applies, with some additional considerations:

Learn about the decision-maker. When pitching outside your company, you may not know in advance all the people from the other side who'll be in the room. To the extent you can, research the company. Learn about the people you know will be present. Get from your contact person any rules of engagement, such as how long you'll have, what kind of presentation materials they're looking for, and how they want you to allocate your time.

Be mindful of your pitch book content and packaging. Your pitch book is the leave-behind material you use to walk listeners through an around-the-table presentation. It could include information about your team, your products and services, your pricing, and your strategy to address this client's needs. Keep the book as brief as possible, paying attention to both substance and style. Boilerplate documents added to create bulk will detract from your essential information. Your pitch prospect may share your book with a competitor, so be mindful not to include what you consider your firm's proprietary or confidential information.

> *As Calvin told Hobbes about his (Calvin's) report, "Bats: The Big Bug Scourge of the Skies," "I've got a secret weapon that will guarantee me a good grade: a clear plastic binder!" People will judge your pitch book packaging before they get to your substance. While snazzy packaging won't assure you a good grade (as it didn't for Calvin), no need to lose points here. Show some style with the look of your book.*

Start the meeting with your proposed agenda and a "process-check" as to time. Confirming or establishing the length of the meeting will help you better allocate available time, reach the key items, and end the meeting on time.

Be likable. Try to make a personal connection. People prefer doing business with friends and with people they see as potential friends. Be warm, self-deprecating, and interested in the prospective client.

Build trust. Trust is the foundation for lasting relationships. Unlike with an internal pitch, this audience doesn't know you well. Be transparent to the

greatest extent possible. Your audience must believe you're open and honest, or at least not withholding material information. If a successful pitch means that a contract will be negotiated later, you may want to raise thorny issues now to resolve them—and build trust in so doing.

Listen for needs and wants. What are the prospective client's must-haves (needs) and would-like-to-haves (wants)? Unlike a pitch to people at your company where you know these needs already, here you must discover them. You may think you know what the client wants, and you may be largely correct. But it's almost certain you don't know everything going on in their world and what would be most helpful to make an effective pitch. Usually prospective clients will tell you their needs and wants if you ask them. Once you know what the prospective client wants, you can then speak to how the products or services you offer will satisfy these wants. As IMG founder Mark McCormack says, "It is so much easier to sell someone what they want to buy than it is to convince them to buy what you are selling."

Listen for objections. Objections probably exist whether voiced or not. Better for you that they are raised so you have a chance to effectively address them and make the sale. Even if your pitch doesn't prevail, you'll at least know why it fell short.

Connect the dots between features and benefits. We've discussed the concept of the audience benefit, which is essential to effective presenting and pitching. Beware pitching the features of your products and services but not making clear the resulting benefits. Speak to how the features you provide will benefit the prospective customer. For example, pitching the depth of your team and the variety of services you perform doesn't provide a client WIIFY. You must add the WIIFY. As part of your preparation for the meeting, think about how you will complete this sentence for every feature: "This will benefit you because . . ." And then demonstrate the benefit by showing how what you have done has benefitted others similarly situated.

Provide case studies. While respecting confidentiality, show what you have done for clients (ideally, well-known ones) as an example of what you can do for this client. Doing so transforms abstract promises into concrete evidence. The more specific and customized you can be about what it is you will do for a prospective client, the more effective your pitch will be.

Differentiate. What makes your company a better choice than the company of the people who presented before you, or who will present after you? Your reputation alone is unlikely to be persuasive. Are you a commodity provider that competes on price? Or is there something about your product, your service, or your track record that makes clear your company is the

best choice, even if that means paying a premium? Know and speak to your differentiators.

Hold your ground. After you've invested much time, effort, and expense into your presentation, you may feel hurt—even embarrassed—to return to your office emptyhanded. But if the terms of the deal offered are unsatisfactory, walk. Don't agree just to agree. Doing so will set you up to fail. Spending time, effort, and expense on a low-profit or loss-leader deal may be a mistake that ultimately will have reputational repercussions when it falls apart. The prospective client has a right to make what you consider to be unreasonable demands. And you have a right to say no and go in search of deals that make more sense—and better clients.

Mind your tongue. Don't bad-mouth people who don't award you their business or who pull their business. Do the best you can to win and keep it, including trying to save it if you realize the business is in jeopardy. But you don't have a lock on anyone's business. Nothing positive is gained by venting your frustration externally. If I'm your client (or prospective client) and I hear you airing your grievances about a current or former client, I assume you'll be talking to others like that about me. Such behavior dents your likability and torpedoes trust.

After we pulled a large service account, the vendor's president embarked upon a phone campaign within our company to bad-mouth the judgment and character of the executive who made the decision and to solicit its reversal. In our view, this behavior confirmed the wisdom of the decision.

Debrief afterward. Win or lose, follow up with the appropriate person on the other side to understand why you won or lost the business. If you won, it's important to know what it was you said or promised that resonated so that you can be sure to deliver on that promise. If you lost, learn why for next time. Maybe there's something you can do about it, maybe not. But you'll have a better understanding of the game you're playing vis-à-vis competitors.

Question and Answer

1. Should I run my idea by my manager before preparing to pitch it?

Decide whether to ask for permission or forgiveness. You're a person of action, and decisions seem to take forever where you work. Why not just implement your idea and see what happens? You might do so if the idea is small in scope and narrowly applicable to your area. Usually, though, to avoid wasting time, and possibly irritating your manager, discuss your idea with your manager and, hopefully, get his approval before proceeding.

Before you discuss an idea with your manager, consider first discussing it with someone who's a reliable sounding board within your company. If possible, consult someone who knows the personalities and who from experience can help you navigate the process and avoid the pitfalls at your organization. This person must be high enough in the company to have a grasp of what the company needs and can afford, but not so high that you're uncomfortable approaching her.

Beware of siloing. This term refers to the actions of people who launch their own roll-outs without communicating with other departments that will be affected. Narrowly focused on their own projects and expertise, those who silo fail to recognize that their objectives are better accomplished by engaging others and deploying broader resources than their own.

Siloing can wreak havoc on a company. For example, the head of IT orders expensive customer-facing technology that the operations team didn't ask for and doesn't want. Or the marketing department rolls out a new customer and vendor payment platform that the accounting department must own and add staff to handle. While well-intended, there's no discussion, no agreement, just unilateral action by one group that affects another group.

We established a 1-800 "We Care" telephone hotline for apartment residents to call if on-site personnel didn't satisfactorily address their concerns. Employees wore neon yellow "We Care" buttons, the toll-free number was widely published, and posters proclaimed: "Speak out. Voice your opinion. [We] want to know." Once the hotline was implemented, most of the calls came from residents who wanted to break their lease without cause, so upper management soon viewed the hotline as a bad idea and had it disconnected. But no one informed the on-site employees about this change in policy. They continued for the better part of a year to wear buttons and hand out brochures. Those calling the "We Care" hotline received a recorded message, "This line is disconnected and no longer in service."

To prevent siloing, discuss with your manager any idea that will affect other departments. Someone, likely your manager, must solicit the support of these departments before the idea is presented to the ultimate decision-maker. This will require going to the right people to discuss the idea and to assess its effect on their team.

2. How much work should I do before discussing my idea with my manager?

Do enough so your pitch piques your manager's interest. When discussing the idea with your manager, expect to pitch and defend it then and there. If you're not ready to do so, your idea may die a premature death. Conversely, if you prepare the idea so extensively that you're ready to pitch and defend it to all audiences, and then run it by your supervisor, he could give you compelling reasons why it's not going to happen. You would have spent a lot of time and effort on the idea for nothing.

The magic is in the middle, tending toward the over-prepare side. Create and learn your elevator pitch. Outline your major talking points. Work through enough of the numbers to be persuasive. Be ready to speak to what work remains to be done to prove the idea and get it in presentable form. Practice what you will say and how you will say it out loud, as before. You must get the idea past your supervisor, even if his direction is to "work it up" (take the next step) so the two of you can meet again to determine if he thinks it's viable. That's a win, since you've received the green light to spend time on the idea to get it ready to pitch.

3. What should I do if I sense I'm losing my pitch?

If it's clear your idea will not prevail, acknowledge this fact and stop. If you persist, you're imposing on people's patience and time. Demonstrate sensitivity to your colleagues by yielding. If unsure how you're doing, carry on and make the best possible case for the idea.

Avoid repeating your arguments. If you've made your case but feel the tide is against you, don't repeat your points as if your audience didn't hear you the first time. A second recitation is unlikely to be more convincing. Such "babbling" reflects desperation and is unpersuasive.

Keep your cool. Know your personal warning signs. Do you feel your face getting red, your forehead getting sweaty, or your facial muscles tightening? Do you hear your volume rising, or a tone of anxiety creeping in? If you can sense your emotions, it's near certain others are perceiving them as well.

> *Once at lunch with a board member, I was defending my choice of insurance broker in response to his suggestion that we consider a different one. He interrupted the conversation to point out that my body posture, tone, and expression indicated I wasn't open to the discussion. Ouch. Try to be aware in the moment (as I was not) of how you're coming across.*

Lighten up to keep your emotions in check. Challenges to your idea are likely business, not personal. Unless you're arguing for a replacement set of defibrillators for the hospital, lives don't hang in the balance if your idea isn't accepted. Maintaining perspective will help you respond less emotionally and more effectively.

4. What if my boss isn't open to my new ideas?

Effective leaders welcome new ideas wherever they come from and trust in their ability to quickly determine whether an idea warrants further discussion. Some leaders, though, are not open to new ideas, at least not from others. A well-known basketball coach supposedly instructed his administrative assistant to respond to fans calling in with ideas: "If you've thought of it, we've thought of it, so no thank you." Click.

Contrast this approach with that of Scotty Bowman, considered the greatest coach of all time in the National Hockey League. On his drive home from work Bowman would listen to sports talk radio—often a wasteland—in case a fan had an idea he hadn't thought of. His humility contributed to his success.

Focus first on your performance. If your idea is met with words to the effect of "Just do your job," consider first how well you're doing your job. The message may not be about your idea, or your manager's willingness to hear it, but rather about your performance. Until your manager views you as performing satisfactorily, she may not be open to hearing your ideas about change. Also consider that her resistance may be a show of annoyance if you're inundating her with new ideas that are inadequately prepared or pitched at inopportune moments.

Consider your big-picture satisfaction with your manager. But for this unwillingness to entertain your ideas, how happy are you with this relationship? Are you learning and growing? Are you treated and paid fairly? Do you want to stay? If your answers are mostly yes, consider hanging in there. Bide your time, at least for now. Over time, you'll likely earn the respect that allows you to be heard by your present manager. Or you'll have a new manager in the ordinary course of affairs who may be more receptive to your ideas.

If you're performing well and are selective about what and when you propose, but your ideas are still unwelcome, you may have a problem. Going above your manager to propose the idea is likely to be poorly received, both by the recipient and your manager when he inevitably learns of it. If, however, this unwillingness to listen to your ideas is yet another symptom of a bad boss, then you may be in an intolerable situation (see "Contribute" and "Advocate").

5. Any final tips and tricks?

Don't dismiss your ideas as unworthy. You may wonder, "Who am I to propose a new idea? I'm relatively new here, or to the industry, so why should anyone listen to me?" Because (1) as a relative newcomer, you may see a solution that those entrenched in doing business the usual way cannot; (2) you may be closer to the problem than others, including your manager, and therefore understand it better; or (3) you may see an idea in a flash of inspiration. Why wouldn't you have good ideas around the work you do every day? You were hired for a reason.

Have the courage to pitch an idea. Many employees aren't sufficiently committed to generate ideas, work them up (perhaps on their own time), and present them to their manager or senior management. Or they're afraid their ideas aren't welcome, won't be considered, or will be dismissed in a disparaging way. No one likes rejection. Safety lies in telling yourself, "I'll just do my job." To be different—and better—take the risk to pitch an idea.

Don't attempt to revise history. Don't claim another's idea as your own. Don't say that you supported someone's idea once it's approved when you didn't (but do get on the bandwagon and enthusiastically implement it as required). And don't deny that you pitched an idea that failed once implemented when you did pitch it. People will notice and think less of you.

Consider these action steps. From easiest to more challenging . . .

- Read a book on selling.
- Read a book on rhetoric.
- Pitch an idea to a civic organization, volunteer group, school, or church.
- Participate in a team pitch at work.
- Pitch your own idea at work.

Lead!

CHAPTER FIVE

"Leadership is the expectation that you can use your voice for good.
That you can make the world a better place."

SHERYL SANDBERG, FACEBOOK COO, AUTHOR

Lead

In many organizations, continued advancement depends on one's ability to lead people. Leadership isn't for everybody and has its pros and cons. It means more recognition by senior leaders, but more scrutiny as well. More opportunity to make decisions and act independently, but more accountability if things go wrong. The ability to hire and promote performers, but the duty to counsel and fire non-performers. The pleasure of delivering the good news, but the stress of delivering the bad news. Being proud of modeling behavior for others to emulate, but risking the humiliation of visibly failing. With the responsibility of leadership usually comes higher engagement, higher rewards, and higher stakes.

Some of you are already leading teams. Some of you may soon be asked to do so. Or you are happy doing what you do now and have no interest in being responsible for direct reports. You may be leading in more subtle ways as you work alongside peers on projects, earning their respect by attitude and ability. Even if you're not interested in a formal leadership role, there is content here that will help you improve your ability to work well with others. Being a leader, whether you're chairing a meeting, heading up a project, or leading a team, requires skills that we all need at one time or another.

If it's not yet your time to lead, use this time to observe those above you. You'll see managers whom you respect and those you might not. It can be difficult to determine just what makes a good leader, but as you'll see, there are specific things good leaders do, and bad leaders don't.

We offer this statement of the leader's job, suitable for framing or writing on your bathroom mirror:

> *My job as a leader is to bring out the best in myself and others to unify my team, develop their skills, and achieve our goals.*

Let's break it down. To be a good leader, you'll need to:

- Bring your best self every day, because you'll be modeling desired behaviors.
- Elicit the best in others, because you need them to do their best work and to push you.
- Unify the team, because your team must work together to accomplish desired results.
- Develop necessary skills, because your team needs them to execute the work.
- Achieve goals, because any evaluation of both leader and team performance focuses on the achievement, or not, of desired results.

What do your team members want from you as their leader? Studies show that "followers" want autonomy, mastery, and purpose. They want freedom to do their work without being micromanaged, the opportunity to develop mastery of something they value, and work they deem meaningful. Many also want connectedness with others and opportunities to advance.

> *Does this fairly describe what you want? As leaders we're all still followers. Even a public company CEO has a board, and small business owners usually have a lender and sometimes investors. Having someone to hold us accountable isn't so bad. The concepts found throughout* Look Out Above! *apply both to following and to leading.*

To meet the expectations of both your manager and team members—and to be an effective leader—you must play three primary roles: culture creator, employee developer, and driver of results. By doing so you will unify your team, develop their skills, and achieve goals, while at the same time address team member needs of autonomy, mastery, and purpose.

Look Out Above! is here to help you develop a personal leadership style that is intentional and effective. You don't need to follow a list of rules, nor adopt a certain style, nor examine the lives of historical figures for leadership lessons. You don't even need to lead the way the person before you did. You can come as you are, since effective leaders fit no mold. You'll lead in a way consistent

with your own style and best skills. Leadership isn't rocket science. People have been doing it a long time, many of them effectively. You can, too.

LEAD ROADMAP

Unify Your Team

1. Make It Matter
2. Set High Standards
3. Build Trust
4. Let People Be Heard
5. Compete as a Team
6. Maintain Perspective

Develop Their Skills

1. Teach
2. Show
3. Delegate

Achieve Team Goals

1. Set Goals
2. Work Your Plan
3. Stay Engaged
4. Decide and Act
5. Give Feedback
6. Ensure Accountability

Unify Your Team

Unifying your team starts with culture. Simply put, culture is what it feels like to work at a place. Items as disparate as compensation, core values, dress code, office design, performance standards, promotion decisions, availability of training, treatment of clients, and workload all contribute to what it feels like to work at a place. As do communications of every kind whether via conversations, emails, or memos, and whether in meetings, in hallways, or on the road.

Different departments within the same company have different cultures depending on who leads them and what they do. Accounting's culture is different from that of Marketing. As a leader, you have an opportunity to shape culture. Your team's culture will reflect you, so your first challenge as a leader is to create a positive one.

Look Out Above!

The importance of culture can hardly be overstated, especially for young professionals. Peter Drucker observed, "Culture eats strategy for breakfast," meaning the best strategy is worthless if a dysfunctional culture can't implement it.

Here are six steps to create a culture that unifies your team:

1. Make It Matter

As a leader, it's your job to connect the dots for your team about why their work matters. Communicate "early and often" how the team contributes to the success of the company and to the financial fortunes of its employees. Are you serving customers and bringing dollars to the bottom line? Are you developing the products that others will sell? Are you providing essential support? Make it clear on a practical level why the success of your team matters to the success of the company.

Also, if you can, address the larger purpose of the company or your team. Most people want to do something with their lives that contributes to the greater good. Simply making money for the shareholders or owners doesn't satisfy. Your company's mission or vision statement—if it has one—may or may not help you here. Link what your company or team does to something aspirational and inspirational that makes people want to go to work in the morning. To resonate with team members, this sense of purpose must feel genuine.

Our apartment property management team directly served both resident and owner customers. It was easy to see our importance to the financial success of the company. What got us more excited was that we were creating "home" for our residents. Home is important to people, and every day we had the opportunity to create something special in their lives: a comfortable retreat, amenities and services that made them feel cared for, and a place where they were proud to live and bring their friends.

2. Set High Standards

Decide and communicate your expectations. Intentionally or not, you're setting standards for your team. Take a moment to think about what standards you have set without meaning to do so. Now think about what you want them to be. Deliberately set standards pertaining to performance, the work environment, values, and anything else that matters to you. Perhaps expectations such as these:

- Achieve individual and team goals.
- Speak candidly to build trust and achieve better outcomes, sooner.
- Disclose bad news and items of concern promptly.
- Be appropriate in language and dress.
- Be honest in all matters, large and small, no exceptions.
- Be on time, meet deadlines, and keep discussion threads moving.
- Be courteous and tolerant, disagreeing agreeably with colleagues.
- Be collaborative and collegial to support each other.
- Work diligently with a sense of purpose.

Help your team understand your expectations so that they can meet them. Consider discussing expectations in a team meeting and providing a standards document that puts them in writing. Reinforce expectations in one-on-one discussions as events warrant.

When we took a real estate company public, the CEO made clear his expectation that we become a great public company that just happened to be in the real estate business. This higher standard raised the bar for all company leaders in terms of performance, disclosure, and transparency.

Live your standards. Day-to-day modeling of desired behaviors is your most persuasive form of influence. What we do matters more than what we say, and as a leader everything you do and say is magnified. Albert Schweitzer observed: "Example is not the main thing in influencing others. It is the only thing." Are your words and actions consistent with the behaviors you want from your team? Are you willing to do what you ask others to do? Do you follow company rules that you insist others follow? Your team is watching and talking about what you do and don't do.

After a hard day's work, Mickey Mouse drops his costume into a chute before leaving the Magic Kingdom. That Disney magic might be lost if Mickey were spotted at 7-Eleven buying cigarettes and beer. You don't get a chute. Regardless of time or place, you're "in costume" whenever a colleague is pres-

ent. Model what you expect from others at work and after work—in the office, in the field, and in the bar.

Enforce your standards. What behaviors are you getting? If no one is meeting your expectations, this suggests: (1) no one is good enough; (2) no one has a clue what your expectations are; or (3) they know but ignore your expectations since they're unreasonable or you don't enforce them. The first option seems unlikely, and the second can't be the source of the problem since you communicated your standards. That leaves the final option, which you can fix. Make sure that your expectations are reasonable. Then, when a team member fails to meet them, provide timely feedback and, where appropriate, consequences.

> *A hard-driving Fortune 500 CEO is quoted as saying, "No one has ever met my expectations, with the exception of my wife." What a master of the universe. Presumably he replaced his leadership team with his wife.*

It's not a bad thing to show genuine anger or frustration once in a great while. While losing a grip on your emotions is usually not helpful or productive, sometimes expressing your anger is warranted—perhaps when a standard you've established has been violated to the detriment and embarrassment of your team. What gives a display of anger or frustration its power is that it's genuine and seldom erupts.

3. Build Trust

Create an environment where team members can do their best work. Employees want an environment that's free of drama and intrigue. For people to work together productively under your leadership, your team must trust you in all kinds of ways. They must believe that you, as their leader, will help them grow their knowledge and skills, and give honest, timely feedback about their performance. They must believe they're being treated fairly and compensated fairly. They also must feel confident that you'll advocate for them and provide opportunities for advancement. In short, they need to trust that under your leadership they'll earn success, recognition, and rewards. Some team members will grant you trust until you disappoint them; others will make you earn their trust.

To earn team member trust, and earn it faster, be:

- Candid—inform team members where they stand so they can make informed decisions.
- Courageous—have the hard conversations and make the hard decisions.
- Loyal—be resolute to the company and to your team.
- Open—reveal something of yourself, and let people get to know you.
- Positive—stay calm and in control, especially when receiving bad news.
- Available—spend time with team members as a team and one-on-one.
- Principled—create a level playing field, a meritocracy without favorites.
- Respectful—treat your team as colleagues.

> *One of the first things I did when taking over a new team was to spend time with each team member to learn about them, including what they did and how they envisioned their future. And to answer their questions and reveal something of myself. The conversation was a two-way street.*

Some leaders, instead of building trust, destroy it. Don't be:

- Absent—missing in action in good times and bad.
- Aloof—being unapproachable and unknowable.
- Arbitrary—making decisions that follow no principle or pattern.
- Disrespectful—berating team members publicly in meetings and group emails.
- Inappropriate—discussing and criticizing team members to their peers.
- Relentless—wearing people down with an unceasing and unrealistic workload.
- Volatile—making people warily read your daily mood, screaming, dropping f-bombs.
- Wimpy—ducking the tough issues and not confronting problem people.

Some leaders "gripe down" by complaining to the team about their pay, their manager, or a new initiative. Some even talk about a job opportunity outside the company they're considering. Such confidences are bad form and destroy trust.

Give team members credit for success. Your team works "with you" instead of "for you." And success was achieved because "they did it" or, together, "we did it." Conversely, as the leader, you take responsibility for failures. Before you assume you have a weak team member, look first to the message or direction you provided or failed to provide.

Appreciate people day-to-day. According to William James, considered the father of American psychology, the deepest need in human nature—one not satisfied by money—is to be appreciated. Give your team members a steady flow of genuine appreciation. Let them know how much they mean to you, and, when appropriate, praise them publicly in meetings and group emails.

Care. Know your team—their aspirations, their spouses, their children, their pets. Ask people how they're doing, and listen to their answers. Be there for people in times of personal stress. Give them space and reasonable time to sort out problems affecting their work. Genuine interest and concern help you deserve and earn trust.

4. Let People Be Heard

We're not talking here about listening to your team members when they approach you to discuss personal concerns or to seek your coaching. That's a given, and part of your job. We're talking about the extent to which you welcome ideas and group discussion, and include team members in your decision-making process. Your objective is to get input and diverse perspectives to make sound, timely decisions that deliver the expected benefit while using a process that develops your team members.

Be open to new ideas. You want your ideas considered, and we've considered steps you might take if your manager refuses to hear them (see "Pitch"). Don't be that manager. New problems or opportunities require new ideas. Ditto for lingering problems you can't seem to solve. Your team may be closer to the opportunity or problem and see things you don't. The best way to encourage team members to express their ideas is to take their ideas seriously and to pursue the best ones. And consider letting the person who came up with the idea play a role in its implementation, regardless of the person's current responsibilities.

Select the best approach for each decision. There are a number of ways to make decisions:

Collaborative approach. You and your team members discuss issues, debate disparate views, and, ideally, reach consensus on how to move forward. You direct a collaborative and transparent process. A collaborative style encourages more and varied input and a lively exchange of ideas among team members. This style hopefully leads to better decisions and execution because team members, having played a role in the process, buy into the decision. They also know the underlying assumptions and the "why" behind the decision. This understanding of the objective allows them to use their judgment and, when they think it's called for, to deviate from the usual approach

to achieve that objective. Encouraging—even expecting—team members to participate also allows them to learn how you think and how a collaborative decision-making process works.

Non-collaborative approach. You make the decisions, alone. This style is quicker and, optimal or not, a decision keeps the business moving. It's also efficient, as it permits team members to stay focused on their tasks. Since you were appointed because of your experience and perceived good judgment, this approach allows you—the person regarded as best equipped to decide—to make the decision. It also ensures accountability, since it's clear who decided.

Your approach. There's a time and place for each decision-making style, with variations along the continuum:

- You decide, without input from others.
- You decide, after soliciting and receiving input from others.
- You lead a collaborative team through a decision-making process.
- You delegate the decision and give feedback and coaching.

> *Consider how you might raise children. Will you make every decision for them? Surely not. You'll determine which decisions are to be made by you, alone, but you'll also let them be heard, to a point. While you want a good outcome, equally if not more important is teaching your children how to make effective arguments and good decisions for themselves. This approach has a place at work.*

You're not presiding over a democracy. You're the leader and are responsible for the decision. Nonetheless, here's advocating that you include your team in the decision-making process as much as possible. Absent compelling reasons—such as confidentiality concerns, lack of time, or a directive from above that you alone make a certain decision—ask your team for input. Listen and see what they recommend, and why. You can make your decision in their presence, or not, as you think best. Doing so provides closure, but you may want time to think on the decision, and, once it's made, you may want to avoid further discussion.

To make a collaborative approach work, filter the decisions that go before your team. Then manage the process, cut off discussion and debate at an appropriate point, and reserve the right to overrule the group consensus if you're not comfortable with it. Using this approach, team members are heard

and, if their position doesn't carry the day, so be it. Once the decision is made, require team members to support it. You remain accountable, even though you chose to make the decision collaboratively with your team.

5. Compete as a Team

Focus outward. It's hard to promote collaboration and collegiality, much less unify your team, if team members feel they're in constant competition with each other. Some businesses—especially sales—seem to have internal competition as part of their DNA.

> *"Have I got your attention now? Good. 'Cause we're adding a little something to this month's sales contest. As you all know, first prize is a Cadillac Eldorado. Anyone wanna see second prize? Second prize is a set of steak knives. Third prize is you're fired."*

Try to minimize internal competition among team members. Instead, aim your team's competitive spirit outward. Compete as a team to achieve team goals and to outperform other teams, both internal (where appropriate) and external (at competing companies).

Match team members with roles. Learn the strengths of your team members to compete effectively, achieve team goals, and to promote their development. Try to find roles where your team members can make the greatest contribution by doing what they do best. The power of teams is in brainstorming collectively to devise better solutions, and in allocating the work according to who does what best. If people can focus on what they excel at, then the team's work product will improve exponentially. For many, one of the great pleasures of leadership is placing team members in roles where they succeed.

Keep the work fresh. When you pursue the same line of business day after day, year after year, things can get stale. Keep the work interesting and your team fresh by taking on new work and new clients, improving your platforms and infrastructure, and, when opportunity allows, bringing in new people with different backgrounds and perspectives. No matter what is achieved, never be complacent—raise the bar and set new goals.

6. Maintain Perspective

Think like an owner of the company. Consistent with "company first," lead as if you own the company, and your financial survival depends on your ef-

fectiveness. If you apply this filter to how you spend your time, build relationships, and make decisions, you'll do fine.

Come to work to solve problems. Without problems, you and your team wouldn't be needed. Believe not only that solutions to every problem exist, but that one solution is better than the others. If you think on the problem hard enough, you'll find a workable solution, even if it's more difficult and costlier, and requires more trade-offs, than you would like.

Lighten up! We can take our work seriously while going about it with a sense of humor. Well-timed, appropriate humor is one of the most important business assets you can have in unifying your team and dealing with the outside world. Some studies suggest the best leaders are those with a sense of humor. In a world of big egos, a humorous, self-effacing comment promotes your likability and lets people know you don't take yourself too seriously. Humor is a great way to create the right atmosphere at the start of a meeting and, when needed, to diffuse tension. If you can point out what is humorous or absurd about a situation, you'll create a bond with others who share your perspective.

Promote loyalty to the company. Just as you are loyal to your manager, expect loyalty from your team. But don't ask or expect them to be loyal to you at the expense of the company—you don't write people's paychecks. Modeling "company first" may sometimes mean absorbing loss by supporting the internal transfer of one of your best team members to another team for the good of the company.

You've now established a culture in which your team functions smoothly, people enjoy working, and the work gets done. Let's focus next on growing your team.

Develop Their Skills

Take ownership of building your team. As a leader you must focus not only on growing yourself but on growing your team. As PayPal director Maria Shi says, "I measure my own success as a leader by how well the people who work for me succeed." Both you and your team have a shared interest in developing their expertise so that over time, team members become more self-directed than you-directed.

Your people will be the primary determinant of your success as a leader. The power of exceptional people on your team is exponential. They exceed your standards, bring new ideas, and attract other achievers. They teach others by word and example. They help the team achieve its goals and create a culture

that ensures long-term success. They challenge everyone—including you as the leader—to be better.

The flipside is also true. The wrong people make it exponentially harder for you to succeed. In a kind but firm way—the way you would want to be treated—you must remove people who for whatever reason aren't getting the job done. By ousting poor performers, you put the "company first" and protect the livelihood of those who are performing.

From your team's perspective, they expect you to teach them something of value. As workers we're all free agents, living on the skills we develop and our ability to find places to use them. People understand the need to develop skills with market value beyond their current place of work. Why would anyone want you to lead if you have nothing to teach them?

And so, your second role as a leader is to develop your people. If you develop their skills, your team members will perform better, and you'll address their need to build mastery. Here's how:

1. Teach

Provide what your team needs to know to be successful. At each position along your way, you determined the skills and knowledge needed to master your job (see "Contribute"). Now, as a leader, do the same for your team. Determine what your team needs to perform at the high level you expect. If company-sponsored training doesn't teach what you want, the way you want, then provide your team the missing training they need. Using an outline, or notes, you might include background information, company-specific ways of doing things, and tips and tricks that work for you. Share stories of what others have done that works. Your team will appreciate your effort, and the impact on both results and morale will be positive.

Many companies bring in outside speakers to address industry "best practices." In my experience, most of these speakers are forgettable. Sometimes we had to "undo" what they said since it was contrary to how we did things (and, of course, no one bothered in advance to ask the speaker what the hell he or she was going to say). The best training came from company practitioners who taught the unique way we did things.

Get help if you can. If you have access to a training department that can help transform your outline or notes into something more, such as a training course, terrific. They may not understand precisely what your team does, much less what you want, so be involved in creating the training product. But the training team does know better than you how people learn and the techniques to best create effective training (such as icebreakers, audience involvement, class materials, spaced learning, and testing). If there is no training team, or if it's unavailable to you, do the best you can.

Leave no one behind. The Pareto Principle suggests we spend 80% of our time on 20% of our people. This 20% will include your weakest performers who need more coaching and the occasional swift kick in the butt. While you must help those in a ditch get out, don't neglect the other 80% who also need your time and attention, particularly top performers critical to the success of the team. Only by being intentional about how and with whom you're spending time will you grow the skills of all your team members and shrink the gap between what they know and what they need to know.

2. Show

Partner with team members to show them how you want things done. Whenever possible, show people what you want by giving them something to look at, such as a marketing piece you consider well done, a document with the structure you want, or a website with key elements of the design you envision. Depending on your work, you may want to let team members tag along and see how you do something. Show them how to make a sales call to a prospective client or a "warm call" to a current client. Or have them listen as you repair a damaged customer relationship, or deal with a non-performing vendor. Let them help you prepare, and watch you give, a presentation or speech, or participate in a negotiation.

After a while, flip roles. You tag along, watch, and let your team member do it. Give timely feedback to help them improve on their next attempt or on their first solo launch.

3. Delegate

Stop doing everything yourself. Your team members have seen you do it and, at some point, they must fly on their own. It's easier of course, at least at first, to do the task yourself. The job gets done quicker, and it gets done the way you want. And you're spared the hassle of back-and-forth discussions with somebody who's trying to do what you already do well. Plus, it's gratifying to the ego to do something well. But continuing to do it yourself doesn't grow your team, and getting bogged down doing other people's work may prevent

you from advancing further in the company. Free yourself by handing off work that others—with training—can do as well as or better than you. As a leader, your gratification will increasingly come from teaching, overseeing, and leading others, and vicariously from the success achieved by your team members.

Delegate projects and relationships thoughtfully. Determine when, what, and to whom you should delegate, including both work assignments and client relationships. You may need to stay involved in some relationships until satisfied the hand-off was successful. Mastery and autonomy are related. The more mastery one achieves, the more autonomy one earns.

When you delegate, don't abdicate. Whether you delegate some or all aspects of a project, check in frequently. Stay constructively involved until you feel your team member can do the job well enough on her own.

> *Former President Ronald Reagan said, "Surround yourself with great people, delegate authority and get out of the way." Then he took a nap. When you think it's best, get out of the way, but don't go away (or nap!).*

Achieve Team Goals

Your company, to defend itself from competitors in the market, and to grow from where it is today, must change. It does so through the process of setting goals. Achieving them determines its success, and, in turn, its ability to support its workforce. As a team leader, your objective each year is to drive results while improving processes. Your challenge is to achieve both financial and non-financial goals for the current period while building the infrastructure necessary to lay the foundation for future goal achievement. The extent to which you do so will affect your performance assessment, bonus compensation, and advancement.

Let's explore your third role as a leader—how to set and achieve goals.

1. Set Goals

Many organizations set corporate, department (team), and individual goals. In hierarchical organizations, the higher one goes up the managerial ladder, the more one's bonus is tied to the company's performance. Lower down the ladder, one's bonus achievement is tied more to team and individual performance.

Organize your goals. Hopefully, your manager will seek your input before your team's goals are finalized. Whether your manager sets your team's goals, or you propose them, or you create them together, consider organizing team and individual goals into three categories:

- Financial—achieve targets pertaining to items such as net income, actual versus budget performance, actual versus prior year performance, margin, number of deals or new accounts.
- Major Business Objectives (MBOs)—achieve non-financial goals such as implementing a new platform, improving stakeholder communication, renegotiating a major contract, making new hires, reorganizing the team, opening a new market.
- Standing goals—complete recurring items such as setting annual goals, holding financial and performance reviews, assimilating new hires, resolving customer issues, making warm client calls, determining team member compensation.

Assign accountability. If no one "owns" a goal, it's unlikely to get done. Every team goal must be an individual goal for someone, so that the completion of all individual goals ensures the achievement of all team goals. If your manager provides only team goals, assign individual responsibility among your team.

Make achievement measurable. The kind of people you want on your team take their goals seriously. They expect to accomplish their goals and be paid accordingly. All goals must be measurable, regardless of whether achievement is assessed on an all-or-nothing basis or a percent-completed basis. If goal achievement can't be calculated fairly, you set yourself up for painful conversations that will damage trust and impair commitment. If the goals provided by your manager aren't measurable, work with your manager to make them measurable.

Decide, when a goal has been set, how you will determine whether and to what extent the goal was accomplished. What will be the measurement criteria and where will you find the data? Since some goals are more important than others, assign a weight to each one. If the sum of all goals equals 100%, what is the achievement of each goal worth? Consider leaving 10% or so unassigned for new goals that might arise during the year.

Communicate goals. Once your team's goals are approved, go over them with your team and build consensus around them. Your team needs to understand the why—why these goals, why they matter to the success of the organization, and why they matter to team members. Ideally, taking their cue from you, everyone buys into the wisdom and relevance of the goals. If you

disagree with the goals, then seek to persuade your manager to change them before presenting them to your team (see "Advocate").

Set deadlines. People respond to deadlines. Communicate deadlines imposed by your boss and set deadlines for remaining goals so that every goal has a specific completion date. Ensure deadlines are not missed on your watch—team member goals are your goals too.

2. Work Your Plan

Now that goals are set, help your team achieve them. Mr. Trammell Crow founded a global real estate empire, and his corporate alumni have launched many other successful companies. His partners recall that he would routinely ask them: "How can I help?" It's a question you too should routinely ask your team members.

Create a plan. Understand the objective—the why of the goal—and create a plan to achieve it. Determine the shortest path you believe will achieve the desired result. Identify the moving parts and the order in which to tackle them. As the COO of Alaska Airlines says, "You just can't tell people to get the airplane out on time."

Perhaps create a flow chart showing the progression of steps: (1) identify all tasks necessary to accomplish the goal; (2) determine which tasks are dependent because a prior task must be completed before it can begin, and which are independent because they may be performed at any time; (3) identify deadlines applicable to both dependent and non-dependent tasks; (4) determine the ideal sequence of steps; and (5) put completion dates for each on a calendar. Some tasks are more difficult than others—pay attention to the most difficult ones. How will they get done, and by whom?

Reinvent the wheel—or not—as needed. The shortest and most effective path to goal achievement may be to use a tool, process, or approach that already exists at your company. Examples include report formats, checklists of every kind, contract language, and established ways to troubleshoot problems, prepare for a negotiation, craft a presentation, or sell an idea. Doing something the way it's expected to be done at your company is efficient, is repeatable, and promotes quality.

But to achieve some goals you may need to be a change agent. Deciding to innovate may be the first step in creating new and better tools, processes, and approaches for the future. Those who challenge established ways of doing things create the breakthroughs, whether in business, medicine, law, sports, or most anything else.

Goal by goal, project by project, give thought to which approach will result in a better outcome. Decide whether an existing tool, process, or approach will work either as is, or as updated, or whether you need to build something new.

Start early and build in flex time. We tend to underestimate how long it takes to do something. Often we don't allow for diversions and unexpected problems that will inevitably arise and slow us down. Start as soon as possible to build momentum and, unless an external deadline prevents you from doing so, add an appropriate cushion (longer than you think necessary) to your time estimate. Set up routines that ensure the team stays on task, and don't let day-to-day problems push you off priorities. Have a backup plan if things don't work out as expected. Assess progress against your plan—busyness doesn't mean effectiveness.

> *Don't be lulled by the calendar. Days matter only if you use them effectively. For big goals required to be completed by year-end, Labor Day is a wake-up call that marks a push to the finish line. The year is two-thirds over, with vacations mostly behind and holidays ahead. Be mindful of where you are on goal achievement and what still needs to be done.*

Clear roadblocks and procure resources. Identify and solve for the "slowest hiker"—people or problems that prevent the rest of the project from moving forward at the desired pace. What if achieving your goal relies on a deliverable by another group, and they are slow or fail to perform? It's your goal and your problem. Figure out how to motivate them or to get the work done without them, even if it means your team doing it. To the greatest extent possible, use your organizational pull to get your team whatever resources it needs to achieve its goals—money in the budget, laptops, tablets and printers, furniture and file cabinets, and supplies of every type. And when a project requires, a bad-ass war room!

Test whether your plan is working. Sometimes your team's plan will work as designed. More often, once set in motion, plans need to be tweaked—or occasionally gutted. Determine at the outset how you'll test to see if your plan is working. Then test and revise as necessary.

3. Stay Engaged

A question every leader has to struggle with is "How engaged—hands-on or hands-off—should I be in my team's execution of its work?"

Decide when, where, and how much you need to engage. Sometimes you'll choose to be detail-oriented. Perhaps because of the importance of an issue, or pressing time constraints, or because someone is struggling. Or because you see that a project is floundering. Beware the temptation to become immersed in detail when supervising a team member who is doing what you did, pre-promotion, because you know the job and are comfortable doing it.

> *Former Disney CEO Michael Eisner apparently insisted that no change be made to Mickey Mouse's costume without his approval. It made sense for him to be involved in the costume details, as Mickey is the iconic brand of the company.*

Other times you'll choose to be more big-picture by providing direction, then stepping out of the way and letting your team execute. You may choose this approach because you think team members will master the subject matter better if they attempt it on their own. Or because, after having been deep in the detail and helping the team "get it," you sense it's now time to step away. Or simply because you believe your time is best spent elsewhere.

You'll use both approaches and, over time, learn when to use which approach. Tend toward the hands-on, detailed end of the continuum on matters you deem critical to team success, and until you know the respective capabilities of team members. By being more engaged, you'll gain deeper subject-matter knowledge, become closer with your team, and get better results.

Hold update meetings. Discuss your intended involvement with your team members, then stay in communication with them to know how they're progressing on their goals against the due dates you set. Allow enough time between meetings for progress, or for lack of progress to be evident and require a different approach. Gravitate to a meeting frequency that for you seems best to keep things on schedule.

Ask questions. Asking questions is your fastest route to knowing what's going on. Former General Electric CEO Jack Welch advises, "A leader's job is to have all the questions. You have to be incredibly comfortable looking like the dumbest person in the room." Even if uncomfortable, ask anyway. Some-

times you want a simple "yes" or "no." Other times you want an explanation. Long questions tend to elicit short answers, while short questions tend to elicit longer answers. If you ask a question and the answer is unsatisfactory, an effective response may be none at all. You may get a better or different answer, or more information, by remaining silent. Also use questions to teach. Help your team members arrive at answers on their own as a result of questions such as why they decided the way they did, and whether they considered certain factors. Asking questions is better for learning—and morale—than telling people what to do.

4. Decide and Act

Being a leader means making more decisions and more important decisions. Your effectiveness depends on the timeliness and quality of your decisions. We're talking about tough decisions, where good arguments exist pro and con for alternative courses of action, where the stakes are meaningful, and where you can't have it both ways. We've already examined the benefits of listening to your team and involving them in the decision-making process. Let's examine how to make better decisions.

Do your homework. Gather relevant information, consider both short- and long-term implications, and be mindful of what precedents your decision will establish. Keep in mind that what you do for one person you'll need to do for another, absent a principled basis of distinction or a willingness to be arbitrary.

Create options. To aid your decision-making, frame issues by establishing the far ends of the continuum of possible alternatives or outcomes. You may not end up choosing one of the far ends, but establishing what they are helps you develop alternatives along the continuum and see where these alternatives stand in relation to one another and to either end (recall "Pitch").

Ben Franklin created a simple decision-making technique. Draw a line down the center of a sheet of paper. List the pros of deciding a certain way on one side, and the cons on the other. According to Ben, "Endeavor to estimate their respective weights," then cross out the items on each side that cancel one another. After reflection, make your decision. Usually this technique will reveal the best answer.

Decide, already! Some leaders adopt a "go-slow" approach to decision-making. These deliberators ponder decisions at length, seek to gather more facts, and keep their options open. At the extreme, deliberators suffer from paralysis of analysis.

Illustrative of a "deliberator" is the late William Clay Ford, former owner of the Detroit Lions NFL team. After another disappointing season, a meeting was set between Ford and then head coach Wayne Fontes. The expectation was that Fontes would be fired. When asked what happened after the meeting, Ford answered: "He didn't quit, and I didn't fire him, so I guess he is still our coach."

Other leaders decide quickly, with whatever facts are available. They don't slow down for fear of making a bad decision, and they don't make "default" decisions by failing to decide. They live by mantras such as "a bias for action" and "any decision is better than no decision." At the extreme, deciders won't sit still to hear the facts and competing considerations. They may fail to appreciate the complexities, the time and resources required, or the implications and unintended consequences.

Illustrative of a "decider" is the athletic director (AD) of an elite college football program who, following a Saturday afternoon blowout loss to a mediocre team, decided that his high-paid, high-drama, low-achievement coach had to go. Not content to wait until the next business day, the AD met the team plane when it landed at 3 am and fired the coach before he could board the team bus back to campus.

Effective leaders use both styles. They consider the cost and other consequences of deciding now versus waiting on more data or input. Here's advocating, unless there are compelling reasons, for your style to be to decide sooner than later and, when possible, now. Likely you'll never have all the information you want. Whatever the realities, by taking decisive action you'll move the business forward, free people to act, and uncover and overcome challenges sooner. Being aware of how long a decision is taking may motivate you to decide.

If you don't decide now, determine what you're waiting for. What do you lack—and that is gettable within your time and cost parameters—to make

an informed decision? Perhaps there is data you need, an opinion you want to solicit, an event that must transpire, or an approval that's required. Once you identify the missing something, determine how to get it, who will get it, and in what time frame. Create a plan with a decision date in mind. You're always in one of two decision-making modes: deciding now or working a plan to decide.

Make your decisions work. Deciding is half the process. The other half is making your decision work. Your decisions will miraculously improve the harder you work to implement them. If your team wasn't part of the decision-making process, inform them of the decision and explain the "why" to help them understand your underlying assumptions and objective. Model a can-do attitude and expect the same from your team.

Change course if you must. Give your decision every opportunity to work and to deliver the expected benefit. When, however, new game-changing information arises or if, despite your best efforts, you can't get the decision to work—and you're now convinced you've made a mistake—take a new tack. Have the courage to reverse or modify your decision.

> *I once participated in an evaluation process where consultants put senior leaders through an intense role-playing hypothetical. I played the manager of a power plant, and the consultants played news reporters who presented facts that increasingly indicated my plant was causing harm. At first, a few people were getting headaches, but any connection to the power plant was tenuous. "Will you close the power plant now?" they asked, to which my answer was no. The facts continued to worsen, and after every new fact I was again asked, "Will you close the power plant now?" If I closed the plant, I had no backbone, and if kept it open, I had no conscience. Don't wait until bodies are lying on the riverbank outside your power plant to reverse course.*

With the responsibility of making decisions comes the certainty that some won't work out as you planned. *The Wall Street Journal* reports almost daily on ill-advised acquisitions, product launches, and investments. Behind each costly mistake lies a "suboptimal" (horrific!) decision. We all make mistakes, and as a new leader you'll likely make your share. Admit the mistake, learn from it, and move on. You can't be a credible leader otherwise.

5. Give Feedback

An important part of your job is giving feedback. Feedback that affirms and changes behaviors is essential to team building. Top performers not only want feedback but say they don't get enough of it. That want to know how they're doing and, in the process, get greater clarity about expectations. They know feedback is essential—to their improvement, greater autonomy, rewards, and career management. Others may need feedback that challenges them to give more effort and do better work to meet your standards. Let the quantity and quality of your feedback distinguish you as a leader. If so, it will be reflected in 360-degree reviews of you by your team.

Give feedback in the moment. Real-time feedback—feedback closely following the behavior observed—works best. Don't tell me the next time my annual review rolls around. Tell me now, while it's fresh. Some say, "praise before and after you give tough feedback." Sometimes known as a "sh*t sandwich," the negative message is bookended by perfunctory compliments. Frequent use renders this tactic transparent, and the praise loses any impact. People need to hear hard messages with or without praise.

New workplace apps make it easy not only for supervisors but for peers and subordinates to provide real-time feedback with "shout-outs," "high-fives," and "praises." Under development is a digital juice box with orange slices.

Provide specifics when you praise or criticize. Not "you did a great job," but "I liked the way you did this, this, and this." Not "This was inadequate," but "Here's the problem with how you handled this." Specific feedback is easier to understand and continues your teaching on ways to improve. Allow room for individuality and develop a sense of what to overlook. Most people expect to be told what to accomplish but prefer not to be told how to do it. The fact that someone is going about a task differently than you would doesn't mean feedback is required.

Hold meaningful performance reviews. If your company has an annual performance review, it's a big deal both for you and your team members. If bonus payments are timed to follow reviews, as is often the case, the reviewee is looking for affirmation and guidance—and bonus dollars. The reviewee expects you to have devoted considerable thought to the review. To meet this expectation and to provide your team members with the benefit of the review process, do the work. Don't parrot back the employee's self-evaluation (weak!) but prepare your own content (hopefully a task made easier by notes

you've made throughout the year). Discuss performance for the period covered, including strengths and areas for improvement, with examples of each.

Once finished, don't put the performance review in a drawer, or send it to HR, and forget about it. You're helping your people grow and building your team. Use your update meetings with individual team members as a forum to discuss progress not only on goals but on performance review items as well.

Give the hard-to-give, easy-to-skip, "last 10%" feedback. It's a pleasure to tell people why and how they're meeting your expectations. When they're not, it's not fair and not helpful to be silent. Should you later terminate a team member's employment, you want him to have been on notice that his performance is subpar and that his job is at risk. Whether in the moment or at review time, give the tough feedback—100% of it.

6. Ensure Accountability

Be understanding yet firm. You've analyzed the performance of your team members and given constructive feedback. Now, how will you deal with poor performers? Will you hold them accountable for the quality and timeliness of their work or will you overlook their poor performance?

We think accountability should be your presumptive approach. If team members aren't held accountable, goals won't be achieved and unwelcome changes will be made, perhaps starting with you. And you'll lose the respect of your team, especially that of high achievers who are demotivated when everyone on the team is treated alike.

But sometimes understanding and a longer-term view are called for. Outcomes are not always within our control, and despite great effort not every goal will be achieved. When you believe the failure to accomplish a goal isn't the fault of your team member, focus your feedback on effort and improvement, not outcome. While you can't minimize the consequences or approve bonuses for unmet objectives, you can continue to believe in and support the team member, for now. Use the approach you believe that the totality of the circumstances calls for.

My first real estate boss—the one who emphasized the link between goal achievement and my continued employment—was an accountability type. After I lost a zoning hearing at City Council, with time, effort, and dollars lost, he got on a plane and came to see me. He didn't come to minimize the outcome, but to show understanding and let me know I was valued. The gesture meant a lot to me.

Conclusion

You now have a blueprint for effective leading—how to unify your team, develop team member skills, and achieve team goals. In so doing, you'll also address team member needs for autonomy, mastery, and meaningful work.

Leadership presents you with a wonderful opportunity if you recognize and act on it. When you look back on your working life, here's betting one thing will stand out: your relationships, particularly your influence on people's lives. Your reflections may bring up memories of how you helped people. Or questions that evoke self-scrutiny—Did I care about them personally, and about their career? Did I give team members candid feedback and help them develop expertise? Was I fair? Did I advocate for my people? Was I supportive of them in times of trouble? In short, was I a positive force in people's lives?

In Dickens' *A Christmas Carol*, Scrooge tells the ghost of Jacob Marley, "You were always a good man of business." The ghost wails in reply: "Business! Mankind was my business. The common welfare was my business; charity, mercy, forbearance, and benevolence, were, all, my business. The dealings of my trade were but a drop of water in the comprehensive ocean of my business!" We believe, like Marley's ghost, that our most meaningful "business" is the difference we make in people's lives. Lead today with a sense of what will matter to you tomorrow.

Application: Meetings

Meetings get a lot of bad press. Some leaders consider meetings a waste of time and take pride in not having them. They look through the conference room window and see seemingly unproductive people sitting there yakking, some with coffee, soft drinks, or snacks. Yipes!

But like it or not, as a leader, you'll spend more time in meetings. At first, you may lament less time to do "real work," but eventually you may come to appreciate that meetings are part of your work. Done right, it's in meetings that ideas are discussed, direction is provided, and decisions get made. Meetings also provide a forum for people to be heard, and contribute to the connectedness that many seek from their work.

> *Me, I'm not so keen on meetings. You may have heard, "A meeting is an event where minutes are taken and hours are wasted." But at times they are a necessary evil, and you will be leading them, so you might as well learn how to do meetings right.*

Airport bookstores sell entire books on how to run a meeting. Here, more briefly, are lessons learned to make your meetings productive and shorter:

Meet as a group only if the need is compelling. Namely, when meeting with people separately is inefficient, and when bringing people together fosters a desired synergy.

Invite on a "need to attend" basis. Your agenda will help you identify those who should be there—those needed to shape the outcome, not those who need to know the outcome (they can get a memo).

Provide an agenda and pre-reading before the meeting. Your agenda will name the start and end time of the meeting as well as list in order the items to be discussed. By providing the agenda in advance, along with any pre-reading, you'll give people time to review, think, and prepare. It's unproductive to ask them to review documents and respond in the moment. Come prepared and insist that others do the same.

Start on time. Your meeting can't start if you're not there. For you to be on time, have the discipline to stop whatever you were doing previously—even if it means leaving your last meeting with unfinished business—and allow enough travel time. Once people discover that your meetings start on time,

with zero delay for stragglers, they'll come on time to avoid the embarrassment of being late. If not, time for a talk.

> *The higher one goes in the business world the less tolerance there is for tardiness. Successful people have busy days full of commitments. Board of Director conference calls start precisely at the scheduled time, with no waiting for late arrivers.*

Assign someone to take notes. Ideally, choose someone who'll do a good job and who appreciates the chance to work with you. Review and edit the notes soon after the meeting while the discussion is fresh. Conclude the notes with decisions made, action steps assigned, persons responsible, due dates, and next steps. If you publish the meeting notes, do so promptly.

Run the meeting efficiently. You called it, so get in, get it done, and get out. Prohibit emailing or texting. To save meeting time, start by summarizing the topic or stating the issue to be decided. Shape the discussion. Call on people and draw in those who are reticent. Rein in dominators and long talkers, and end off-topic discussions. Notice and thank those contributing. Create a "parking lot" of topics identified during the meeting to be dealt with later. End on time.

Follow up on action items and due dates. If a follow-on meeting is held on the same topic, the notes from the prior meeting become the basis for the agenda. You may prefer to organize your agenda into "old" and "new" business, with old business being a review of progress on action items from the last meeting. Those who haven't done what they were assigned will start scrambling when your next agenda arrives in advance.

Review standing meetings regularly. Avoid meeting-creep by periodically evaluating the productivity of standing meetings. Can they be eliminated? Shortened? Combined with another meeting? Or held with fewer or different invitees? If you have something akin to a Monday morning staff meeting, are you getting the benefit from it you envisioned? Are you in and out in a half-hour or less? How can your meetings be improved?

Everything we've said to this point about running meetings also applies to running conference calls.

Move the meeting venue for special occasions. When seeking fresh ideas, consider going somewhere fresh. Strategic planning or brainstorming sessions may be more productive offsite.

Question and Answer

1. How do I get better at difficult conversations?

Don't shy away from having them. Difficult conversations are the uncomfortable ones, including those where you tell people they aren't performing or you're letting them go. Few leaders enjoy these conversations, but they come with the job. The more you have hard conversations, the less intimidating they become. Hold them in person—not by phone or email. Talk in a calm, conversational voice, with emotions in check. Be guided by two principles: put the "company first" and treat people the way you wish to be treated.

Prepare. As in much of business and life, preparation is the key to less stress and better outcomes. If you're initiating the conversation, consider creating a document that enables you to cut, paste, and rearrange thoughts as you prepare. Script the conversation you anticipate: your talking points, the response you expect from the team member, your reply to that response, and next steps. Organize your thoughts into logical groupings—perhaps the person's conduct, its impact on the organization, and the consequence to him. Put key points in their desired order. Make notes for reference to make sure you cover everything during the conversation.

If you initiated the discussion, control it. When you meet, start by telling the team member why you called the meeting. If he already knows its purpose, restate it anyway. People who are apprehensive about losing their job aren't good listeners. So take that subject off—or put it on—the table. For a counseling session: "Bill, we're here to talk about improving your performance." For a termination, "Bill, the decision has been made to let you go." Or, if you prefer the active voice that places responsibility, "Bill, I've decided to let you go." Then:

1. Deliver your message. Focus on the behavior, not the person. Pair negative behaviors with negative consequences, and positive behaviors with positive consequences.
2. Listen. Let the other person be heard—completely and without interruption. Perhaps take notes to ensure you address key points when you respond.
3. Respond. When you prepared, you anticipated what you thought the person would say. You should expect most of what you hear.
4. Discuss next steps. After you have spoken, listened, and responded, discuss what happens next. What must change, by when, and how will you evaluate?

For a termination, be kind, firm, and brief. The decision has been made, so extensive discussion with the person you're letting go isn't productive. Treat

the person as you would want to be treated. Use language consistent with the legal theory of the termination (position elimination, poor performance, something else). Likely your company requires a third person to sit in for a termination or serious counseling (such as putting someone on probation) to ensure a witness hears what is and isn't said. Even if no witness is required by policy, bring someone from HR or your manager to protect yourself from false charges.

Following yet another scandal, a well-known college basketball coach about to be placed on unpaid leave met with the college president. The coach's driver circled the parking lot and didn't even park. A brief conversation was correctly anticipated.

If you didn't initiate the discussion, listen first. Conversely, a team member may initiate the hard conversation. He or she isn't enjoying the work, is being sexually harassed, or has problems with your leadership. The possible topics are many. Listen attentively and without interruption before you ask questions or comment. You'll be better able to respond, and your team member, after having been heard, will be better able to listen.

2. I just lost a strong contributor. What do I do?

It hurts to lose a key contributor who makes your team better. You might even think you can't do without her. You can, and must.

Try to avert this problem before it starts. Know who your best people are and do all you can to take care of them (see "Advocate"). Make it hard for them to leave by getting in front of issues such as compensation, autonomy, and opportunity for advancement. Recognize that it's challenging to retain entrepreneurial people whose ultimate objective is to do their own thing. For these people, keep them as long as you can as you help them develop their skills. When they're ready, do what you can to help them launch.

Find someone better. Despite your best efforts, expect someday to lose someone you consider special. When that valuable team member moves on, adopt the attitude that no one, however exceptional, is indispensable. If you're able to replace her, view it as an opportunity to get someone better, or at least someone as good, only with different qualities and personality traits. Project the attitude that being at your company, and on your team, is special and desirable. Your belief that you'll find a suitable replacement will prove helpful if a key contributor makes demands (such as compensation) you cannot or will not meet.

3. I have permission to make a hire for my team. Any thoughts?

If you get the chance to hire, make the most of it. To do so:

Create a profile. Identify the skills and competencies you're seeking, including must-haves and nice-to-haves. You can't listen for them in an interview if you haven't identified what they are.

Listen and look for behaviors. Behavior reveals the truth. Don't tell the candidate the skills and competencies you're looking for. If you do, be skeptical of what the candidate says he's good at (hint: it will be whatever you said you need). Look instead at what the candidate has done—his body of work—to reveal what he can do. Push for information about what he does at his present employment, and what he's accomplished that's noteworthy. Ask about accomplishments at past jobs, during gaps between jobs, and outside of work. Ask about times of adversity—how he coped, what he learned from it, and how he has applied lessons learned. Successful people learn and gain confidence from trying experiences that make them realize they're capable of more than they thought.

Pay attention to attitude and energy. What is the candidate's energy level as she describes her behaviors? What does she talk about, especially when she initiates the topic? What seems to excite her? Recognize that you're seeing candidates on their best behavior because they want something from you. Any hint of issues now—an inability to succinctly or directly answer a question, an exaggerated sense of self-importance, a lack of self-awareness, a flippancy about ethical issues, an inappropriate use of humor—will be exacerbated if you hire the person.

Identify prior supervisors. It's a safe bet that anyone listed as a reference will have good things to say about the applicant. Talk to them if you wish. More importantly, and without regard to whether the person is listed as a reference, learn whom the candidate reported to at every place of employment listed in his résumé. Ask for contact information (even if the candidate must provide it after the interview) and permission to call them. If you later check references, be sure to call these people (and hope they will talk to you). The candidate's reaction after you ask for this information may be revealing by itself.

Don't settle. Even if the hiring process takes more time than you'd like, adopt the view of "short-term pain, long-term gain." Suffer the stress of working without a full team until you've thoroughly uncovered and vetted candidates so that eventually you add the best candidate to your team. That candidate may already have the skills you need, or may be deficient in some way, but you're convinced that she's a "great athlete" who'll be a quick learner with upside potential.

4. How do I lead people older than I am?

This situation may feel awkward both to you and to the senior, more experienced employee.

Consider giving more space. Hopefully the employee has developed expertise and needs less coaching. Experiment with providing less direction, but be the leader you're paid to be. Set goals, ensure accountability, give feedback, and all the rest. The senior worker still wants a positive relationship with you and expects you to have something of value to teach.

Insist on respect. Successful people lead with confidence. You've been selected to lead, so trust the judgment of those confident of your abilities. Trust too your own judgment. Accept the mantle and act the part. How you carry yourself is important in getting others to follow. Your leadership will reflect your own style. Don't apologize for it or tolerate disrespect. If you perceive resentment from someone who perhaps envies your leadership position, that's their personal problem, but you need to confront it. Hold a difficult conversation to address the bad attitude.

5. Should I create an award program for my team?

An award program can help unify and grow your team. Recognizing high achievers reinforces the standards you set, shows that your standards are doable, and rewards your best people. It may even motivate others who, not recognized, also want a "Pin from the Pope."

If your company's award program doesn't address your team's needs, ask your manager for permission to create a custom one. If approved, collaborate with your HR department to create your award program (if your organization has an HR team you can access). Since you know best the behaviors you want recognized and the source of the underlying data to prove out the winners, don't delegate to, but instead partner with, HR. Ensure the awards you propose don't conflict or compete with company awards.

Awards take more time and attention than you might think. Awards must motivate the right behaviors. They should also be based on compelling data to ensure excitement over the choice of winner. With this in mind:

- Set objective versus subjective criteria—awards should be data-driven based on measurable performance. Bill can't win a trip to the Bahamas because a teammate wrote in an email that "He's always there for his customers."
- Spread your award budget to more people by giving more small awards rather than a few large ones. Don't hand out a trip abroad, a new car

or truck, or a large cash award. Award something tangible and, ideally, something that the recipient can proudly display (but please, no silly plaques or certificates!).
* Recognize winners in front of the team—ideally away from the office and with your manager and other luminaries present.

6. Any final leadership tips and tricks?

Learn from leaders around you. It's unlikely your manager will sit you down and say, "This is how you should lead." Instead, learn by observing and incorporating into your leadership style behaviors you find worth emulating—and by rejecting those you don't. When your time comes to lead (if it hasn't come already) you'll draw upon your observations. In the same way, your team is learning leadership skills by observing you.

Mind your metrics. When you get the opportunity to influence what gets measured, particularly for your team, be mindful to measure only what matters. As companies become more data-driven, the number of metrics tends to increase. Too many items—or the wrong items—get measured. These metrics carry a cost to produce, and a cost to review. Finding the right metrics is often not obvious, or easy. Here's one test for an effective metric: Will the results cause you to do anything different? If not, why bother with it? Track and focus on the few metrics that matter, those that dictate action.

Document lessons learned. Following the conclusion of every major project, before moving on to the next big thing, document the lessons you learned from the experience (as you did after you pitched an idea). Put your thoughts in a database where they will be available to those who come later. This discipline may pay dividends in the future—recording the lessons of the past will enable others to repeat what worked and avoid prior mistakes.

Go see people if you lead teams in the field. People need to know who you are, what you care about, and that you're paying attention to them. Phone calls and emails alone won't build relationships.

Go see people if you're in charge of maintaining customer relationships. Just because a customer isn't complaining doesn't mean he's satisfied, or feels appreciated, or isn't looking to replace you. Go see your customers on a timely basis. Get feedback and build relationships. Express appreciation for their business and their trust in you and your team. If you lose an account, the first thing you'll be asked is, "When did you last go see them?"

Form a conversation club. With your manager's support, identify leaders at your level in other companies in your industry—ideally ones with whom

you're not in direct competition—and establish a meeting schedule to discuss ideas and industry issues. Set an agenda in advance, with each person contributing topics he would like to discuss. The club won't last forever, and will naturally terminate as its usefulness declines or as its members move on (or as the companies represented merge!). But you'll gain valuable insights, including the realization that your competitors are as smart and focused as you are.

I was part of a four-person conversation club of young leaders from companies serving different geographies throughout the country. We hatched the idea at a conference. We met three or four times a year and rotated the meeting place to each person's office. What made it work was the give and take, and the trust that developed among us. To get ideas, each person felt obligated to give ideas. And while people were careful not to reveal confidential information, confidences were respected.

An alternative is to find leaders at your level in your city who are in different industries. While the industry connection is lacking, you'll face similar issues and benefit from different perspectives. Such a club might already exist, and if so, perhaps you can join it. If it doesn't exist, consider starting one.

Advocate!

CHAPTER SIX

"You can't always get what you want. But if you try sometimes, you just might find, you get what you need."

THE ROLLING STONES

Advocate

Advocate means "add a voice." Namely, your voice, asking for something not yet offered or given. If you don't ask for what you want and, when necessary, stand up for yourself, there's a good chance your outcomes will be less than they could be. The sponsor of a well-known seminar on negotiation says, "In life you don't get what you deserve, you get what you negotiate." Since no objective standard exists to reveal what one deserves, we could transform his statement to say, "In life what you negotiate is what you deserve."

At work, you need to speak up to get:

- Increased compensation
- A promotion or new title
- Work that's more interesting and challenging
- A bigger role, a move to another department, or to report to someone else
- A team to lead or join that's pursuing a new initiative
- Flexible hours, less travel, or the ability to work from home
- An education allowance or funding for your MBA
- Your manager ceasing to engage in certain behaviors

We're talking here about advocating for yourself and—if you're leading a team—for others. The possibilities of what you might want and ask for are many. It is said that "everybody wins" in a negotiation in which agreement is reached. The reality isn't so sanguine. Most negotiations, even "soft" ones between employer and employee, result in better deals for some and worse deals for others.

6

Many people don't ask for enough. They settle for less than they're worth and less than they could get. As novelist Nora Roberts says, "If you don't go after what you want, you'll never have it. If you don't ask, the answer is always no." You're not without bargaining chips since businesses need good people, and people who contribute are hard to attract, recruit, and retain. While the timing of the economic cycle is not irrelevant, those who contribute usually have some leverage—if properly applied.

I've been conducting a partnership negotiation case in my MBA classes at UNC for over ten years. Students arguing from identical facts get widely disparate results. Most students are satisfied with their outcome until they learn what others similarly situated achieved. To receive, you must ask.

Which isn't to say that you can't ask for too much. Some young professionals "pull on a rope not tied," meaning they make demands assuming incorrectly they're doing so from a position of strength. They over-estimate higher-ups' perception of their contribution and willingness to accommodate them. An ability to accurately perceive your reality is required.

Summer interns at a Fortune 500 company decided the firm's dress code was "overly strict" and unfairly enforced, particularly as it pertained to footwear. Unaware that firms often view interns as an unfortunate but necessary part of the recruiting process, all but one intern signed a petition requesting proposed dress code modifications. The company fired all interns who signed the petition.

Small but frequent demands tend to untie one's rope over time. A particularly egregious demand may untie it in one fell swoop.

How do you make sure your rope stays firmly tied, while still getting what you want or need? Contribute first, then advocate. More leverage exists for those who contribute and are perceived by those above as contributing. Recall one of the commandments painted on the barn in George Orwell's *Animal Farm* (as later revised by Napoleon and his fellow pigs): "All animals are equal, but some animals are more equal than others."

Employees are treated differently in terms of compensation and advancement opportunities. Perhaps you add so much value that your boss and others are

already discussing—without prompting from you—how to ensure that you don't test the job market. Regardless, whatever it is you're asking for, and whether it's on your behalf or on your team's, we're here to help you leverage your contribution, preserve your long-term prospects, and give yourself the greatest chance to obtain the outcomes you seek.

Although these advocating principles apply to any request, we'll focus on three important ones to ensure that (1) you're not caught under a crushing workload that lowers the quality of your work, or with a steady diet of uninteresting work, or between the demands of multiple managers; (2) your accomplishments are known, and you're considered for opportunities of interest to you; and (3) you're paid fairly. If you apply the principles that follow, you'll have added your voice to obtain for you or your team something not yet offered or given.

ADVOCATE ROADMAP

Understand the Game
 1. Be Low Maintenance
 2. Assess Your Contribution
 3. Advocate Gently

Advocate for Yourself
 1. Manage Your Workload
 2. Pitch Your Performance
 3. Ensure Fair Compensation

Advocate for Others
 1. Defend
 2. Shield
 3. Champion

Understand the Game

Let's first consider three concepts that underlie all of your advocacy discussions:

1. Be Low Maintenance

Don't be needy. Be someone who doesn't require constant attention, affirmation, or reassurance. Early in your career is not the time to be needy. Neither is later, for that matter, but by then you may have earned more goodwill.

Some executives see opportunity when non-performers make demands. They hope that when these demands aren't met, the employee will quit and save the company the aggravation of terminating and the cost of paying severance.

If in doubt, don't make demands. When you do, you're inviting an assessment of your contribution, and you may not like the outcome. Sometimes those who make demands are told, "Not no, but hell no." If you hear such a reply, say "never mind," apologize, and scurry back to your work station. Later you can work to mend fences.

Even strong contributors who make constant demands become tiresome and eventually risk losing the goodwill and support of their manager. They survive if they're deemed "net accretive," meaning that on balance their positives outweigh their negatives. Being perceived as someone who is both performing and low-maintenance is a source of power in any discussion when you ask for something personal. That you don't ask often means more when you do. People will be more likely to help you.

Develop a sense of what you can ask for and when. You didn't create the workplace world you live in, but you need to understand it. When you do pull on the rope by advocating for yourself or others, act in a way that's consistent with your company's culture. Some companies (both for- and non-profits) are a "kinder, gentler" place to work. They've strayed from "company first," and celebrate loyalty and tenure above performance. Other companies are tougher. They expect and demand performance. They live the "company first" mantra, viewing every decision through the objective lens of "what's best for the company." Although the practice seems to have diminished, some companies even "force rank" their employees annually and cull those at the bottom.

At some companies the unwritten rule is "We negotiate hard externally, and harder internally." Meaning that while the company conducts tough negotiations with outsiders, the most difficult ones are among insiders when dividing up the company's pie. If you're going to live in a "Trust me, I won't screw you unless I need to" world, it's best to know it.

Know the rules. In hierarchical companies the "rules," both written and unwritten, vary greatly. Before becoming eligible for a promotion or pay raise, you may, for example, be required to serve in one position for a required length of time or complete designated training. Rules are made to be broken

by exceptional people, but it's best to know what they are at your company. Conversely, in a small-company culture there may seemingly be no rules, but those who don't advocate for themselves may languish.

2. Assess Your Contribution

Whether it's a large, hierarchical company or a small, flatter one, it's important to see yourself as those above you do. It's prudent to do so even if you're not advocating for something, but critical if you're about to raise compensation or other matters. Most employees don't honestly assess their contribution, but their managers do.

Consider your replaceability. In a business context, no one is indispensable, and everyone is replaceable (see "Lead"). Some, though, are more readily replaceable than others. Do you bring something unique to the company that makes you difficult to replace? If your presence and contribution were removed, would the work of the firm falter, at least for a while? Do you have some special expertise? Can you sell, market, or service clients? Can you write code? Do you add to bottom-line revenues? Do you lead teams effectively? A vague assertion that "I have people skills" is unpersuasive. A grasp of your present reality, whatever it is, will influence the way you advocate. The more replaceable you are, the more lightly you must tread.

Consider your cost. One element of replaceability is cost. For those of you who work for others, someone has calculated your "all-in" cost—salary, bonus, benefits, and overhead load.

At private companies, the people watching the payroll are the owners. Every dollar paid to you, or expended on your account, is a dollar that doesn't go to them. Even a large and growing pie is still a pie. A slice for one cannot be a slice for another, and the owners know it.

At public companies, senior management watches the payroll on behalf of the shareholders. The connection is less personal, as a dollar paid to you doesn't directly reduce the compensation of those at the top (which explains why public companies often pay more than private ones for the same position). But public companies must report overhead, and answer to shareholders and analysts.

You may create value in ways that cannot be measured by dollar production, but at least be mindful that your presence carries a cost, and that someone above you knows what it is and is assessing if you're worth it. What is your cost?

Consider the dollar value of your contribution. Do this to manage your own career, not to share with others. For the math to work at for-profit companies, some if not most employees are expected to produce revenue significantly greater than their cost. If everyone just covered their cost, there would be no profit, and thus no incentive for the owner to keep the enterprise going. Revenue producers are needed to feed the owner and big dogs at the top, and to cover the cost of those in support positions.

> *At my first real estate job, every transaction I initiated generated fees—acquisition, construction, property management, asset management, and, later, disposition fees. I shared in none of these. I earned a salary and maybe a cash bonus. I was there to make money for the owners of the company in excess of my cost. And I was grateful for the opportunity to do so. It's how the working world works.*

Can you estimate the dollar value of your contribution? If so, how does that amount compare to your cost? If you're a producer, that dollar value could be solely attributable to you or, if you're a leader, to the value created by you and your team.

But, you say, "I'm in Accounting (or Human Resources, or IT, or Investor Relations, or Marketing). I don't produce revenue, but support those that do." You're certainly not alone. Those in staff jobs indirectly make revenue generation possible by supporting line jobs that directly generate revenue. But keep in mind your reality. Since you're not producing revenue, someone else must produce revenue to cover their cost and your cost, as well as profit. This makes both you and members of your support team more vulnerable. When tough times come, staff positions are often first to be cut because of the indirect connection between them and revenue production.

What to do then if you or your team is in a support role? This reality is no reason not to do work you love, but realize it's even more imperative that your contribution be recognized, and that others appreciate your value to the organization.

3. Advocate Gently

When you're ready to ask for something:

Set written goals. Studies show that in negotiations (and in life) people with high aspirations get better outcomes. Those who set goals—written goals and

high goals—achieve more. Writing down goals brings them more sharply into focus and serves to motivate you to make them happen—you're making a commitment to yourself. So think about and write down specific "asks" from your boss for yourself or, as a leader, for your team or for a team member.

An advertisement for Post-It Notes states that "you achieve 42% more when you write it down." Hard to write much on a Post-It Note, but the point is well taken.

Create a plan. Achieving better outcomes starts with planning. If the first time you think about how to phrase your ask is just before you sit down with your manager, you're not likely to be pleased with the outcome. Time and effort spent preparing should be proportional to the importance of the discussion. If you care greatly about the outcome, prepare accordingly. Like anything that involves work, once you start in earnest and make progress, your stress level will go down and your enthusiasm will go up. Momentum resulting from action turns fear of the unknown into energy and progress.

Do your homework. Command of the subject matter of your upcoming discussion is key to risk reduction. Identify the information holes in your plan and determine how to fill them. Spend the necessary time to gather information. If, for example, the discussion is to be about your compensation, you'll want to know the likelihood of your finding a similar or better job in a reasonable time and at what compensation.

Your preparation should anticipate likely responses to your request and devise strategies to address them. Should you want a pay increase, for example, you might hear objections like these: your performance doesn't justify it; the company can't afford it; you're already paid at the top of the range for your position. Or, come back some other time (but go away now!).

Be prepared for your requests—and for you—to be dismissed. Be ready with your most persuasive reasons why your request is reasonable. And develop alternatives. What if you can't get what you ask for? Are there other outcomes that might satisfy you, and how attractive, and likely, are they?

Do a dress rehearsal. As if preparing for a presentation, practice. Hear yourself saying the words you plan to speak. Assess how you come across. Record yourself, or get feedback from a friend.

A friend was nervous before asking his crusty boss for a raise. When he summoned the courage to make his request, he stuttered out, "I would like a rais-in." His boss, acting like this was the funniest thing he'd ever heard, seized on the fumble. "Raisins? You want raisins? I'll give you raisins!" My flustered friend quickly departed without getting what he'd come for. Practice before you pitch.

Negotiate cooperatively. Discussions about your performance or opportunities for advancement are not adversarial. Instead, at their best, these discussions are collaborative as you and your boss seek a solution that works for you both and that furthers the relationship. Even if the topic is money, think of your conversation with your manager as more of a discussion than a negotiation.

Discussions with people with whom you expect to have a continuing relationship call for cooperative tactics: making reasonable demands, engaging in give and take, creatively exploring options, being sensitive to feelings and to how you're coming across. Threats and emotional tactics—anger or pouting or crying—have no place here.

When former Soviet Premier Nikita Khrushchev gave his "we will bury you" speech at the United Nations, he became so enraged he banged his shoe on the table. A photo showed he was wearing a shoe on each foot at the time. Somebody with the power to destroy the world comes to a meeting with a shoe in his pocket to deliver a threatening rant. Scary, as intended. Probably best not to use this shoe ploy when you meet with your manager.

Regardless of your ask, be it for more money, a flexible work schedule, or a shower so employees can bike to work, you hope there's some give and take with your manager and not "This is what it is—take it or leave it." While exceptions exist, particularly in fields where top producers are routinely poached by competitors, it's difficult to be adversarial with your manager and maintain an effective working relationship.

If you're naturally cooperative, you may need to push yourself to ask for what you want and think is right. If you're naturally competitive, remember the big picture (maintaining your relationship and keeping your job) and dial it back a bit. Your personality will always influence the way you go about ad-

vocating, but knowing your preferred style will help you push yourself or, as needed, restrain yourself to obtain your desired outcome.

Use advocacy to build relationships. View the advocacy process as an opportunity to build your relationship with your manager. Show a command of the issues, including ways to resolve conflicting needs. Make clear your loyalty to the company and desire to make a difference.

Advocate for Yourself

With these underlying principles in mind, let's look at three common, and important, issues that might require your advocacy skills.

1. Manage Your Workload

Too much work. There's only so much you can do to influence your workload, but having too much to do will make it hard for you to do your job well. A study of five thousand managers and employees found that the highest-ranked performers mastered the art of "selectivity." Whenever they could, highest-ranked performers determined "which priorities, tasks, meetings, customers, ideas or steps to undertake and which to let go. They then applied intense, targeted focus on those few priorities in order to excel." The study found that in terms of performance, selectivity mattered even more than talent or hard work.

This finding should come as no surprise. The quality of your work is unlikely to be a differentiator if you labor under a constant and crushing workload. You must advocate for a workload that allows you to do your best work without being perceived as a slacker. Being thoughtful about what you take on is unrelated to your work ethic. You'll work hard in any event; you'll be more effective if you spend time on what you judge matters most, and if you're able to devote adequate time to the task.

To the extent you can, then, be selective about what and how much you take on. If workload is a problem for you, have a candid conversation about it with your manager. Get his help to determine priorities and to cut non-essential work from your to-do list. As always, talk in terms of "company first"—how it's imperative that you do quality work and achieve your goals. The alternative is to quietly bear the overload, while your resentment builds, your work suffers, and the perception of your ability shrinks.

Too little work. Workload at most companies ebbs and flows, but the ebbs are typically of short duration, as are, hopefully, those crisis moments requiring intense focus and commitment. Given that rationality will ultimately prevail (see "Contribute"), a workload that is continuously light is unsustainable. It

also does nothing to help you climb the learning curve or allow you to differentiate. Ask for more work carefully: "I would like to take on more" versus "I don't have enough to do." Despite your good intentions, if you advertise your lack of work too loudly or broadly, you may find yourself redundant.

Uninteresting work. If your work is boring, ask for more interesting work. You realize that most jobs have tedious aspects. New lawyers, for example, seem to spend years collating documents—which may be one reason you chose not to be a lawyer. But if, after a reasonable time, you think that too much of your job is busy work, you'll need to speak up using your advocacy skills. It will be hard for you to be committed—much less fulfilled—if you have a seemingly unending diet of grunt work. This monotony could explain why, per one study, "some 43% of young workers are poised to quit within two years." Your odds of being assigned challenging work will improve if you come in with suggestions about the work you'd like to do.

Too many managers. It's not unusual to report to two managers, or to report to one manager but have multiple people assign you work. A challenge arises when your higher-ups assign you tasks without communicating with each other and without prioritizing their work vis-à-vis each other. You're in the middle, trying to decide what matters most and which one to please first. It's a difficult situation to be in. No matter—it's you who must solve it. You can't allow yourself to please one person but not another, or please neither. You can expect that anyone who assigns you work will be consulted about your performance at review time, if not before. For your career to move ahead, all such persons must be enthusiastic about the quality of your contribution.

If you have multiple managers, or multiple people assigning you work, and you must manage conflicting priorities and deadlines, you can:

- Rely on your ability to gauge what matters most to each person and then prioritize your work. This may prove effective for a while, depending on how well you correctly gauge priorities. Those funneling assignments to you will like it, since your method of prioritizing doesn't involve them. But you risk misjudging priorities and disappointing someone. If you pursue this option to the exclusion of others, inevitably you'll choose incorrectly.
- When conflicts arise, engage in shuttle diplomacy by going to your managers, separately, to clarify what matters most to them and by what date they need it. Then prioritize your work. This option has the advantage of making your managers aware of your predicament and helping you clarify what is and isn't urgent. Managers may try to be gracious, when they can, by allowing you to put another manager's priority first. Or not, which may create problems for you.

- Call a meeting with all managers to explain the demands on your time and ask those assigning you jobs to work together to prioritize your schedule. This option makes your managers aware of your predicament and asks them to solve it. Taking this step also says something about your initiative and problem-solving ability—you're trying to make the company function as smoothly as possible while supporting your colleagues' careers as best you can. Hopefully after such a meeting they will volunteer to work together going forward to make clear your priorities or devise some mechanism to solve the problem. The disadvantage of this approach is that it takes time from those who assign you work, which they may resent if they feel you could have determined the conflicting priorities on your own.

Since you'll likely use all three options at one time or another, experience will guide you as to when to use which approach. Calling a meeting will likely be your last resort, to use only when you're overwhelmed.

What if your manager's boss sends work to you directly—without informing or cc'ing your manager? Unless this is a normal practice where you work, you may want to inform your manager. Otherwise, you risk her discovering she's been cut out of the communication loop. She may incorrectly believe that you've gone around her to her boss, and her misperception may damage your relationship. Your disclosure to your manager properly puts the burden on her to deal with the situation.

2. Pitch Your Performance

Performance reviews are important. At most organizations they occur once —maybe twice—each year. Some firms have eliminated them. If so, don't hesitate to ask for a review once or twice a year. To make the most of your reviews:

Have an agenda. You need certain things from your performance review. Seek to:

- Get a sense of where you stand with the company.
- Learn behaviors of yours that are viewed as positive, and any that are not.
- Determine your future in the company's plans—department and role.
- Set or confirm goals for the upcoming year.
- Address compensation matters.

- Get answers to any questions you may have.
- Float your aspirations and see how they land.
- Understand, where applicable, next steps.

Document your accomplishments. Your past accomplishments may be the best indicator of your future accomplishments, as well as your ability to help your manager achieve his goals. Don't merely hope that your manager is aware of your accomplishments—ensure that he is. Whether or not such a list is required, document your accomplishments for the period under discussion.

Some might believe that your work should speak for itself and that you shouldn't try to demonstrate to your boss or anyone else the merits of your performance. Noble thought, perhaps, but nonsense when it comes to your performance review. Your manager is unlikely to remember all the ways in which you contributed over the past year. Your review is your best opportunity to make your manager aware of your contribution.

If your company requires you to complete a self-review, it's your opportunity to provide accomplishments. If not, provide them in a free-standing document in advance of your review, ideally before bonus amounts are decided. Don't assume your manager will read it in advance; bring copies for both of you. Keep a running file of your accomplishments through the year so that at review time (or whenever) you can easily create a polished document.

List agreed-upon goals and their achievement. If you didn't achieve a goal, acknowledge it. Don't inflate your accomplishments Avoid "weasel words" that are evasive or make a statement that's almost-but-not-quite true—for example, claiming a goal to be "more or less" achieved, or a project's completion "slightly" delayed. If bonus calculations are prorated (versus all or none) for goals less than 100% achieved, provide a proposed percent completion—and the basis for your numbers.

Divide accomplishments into logical buckets. Use subheaders. Prioritize items within the buckets, starting with those having the most impact. When you can do so fairly, determine the dollar value of an accomplishment.

In my experience accomplishment submittals often arrive as an unorganized, lengthy list of bulleted items. A list is easier to follow and more compelling when each bulleted accomplishment is organized by topic, starts with a verb, and is placed in an intentional order within each subheading. Recall our discussion of the proper way to construct a list (see "Write"). A better list equals a better performance review . . . and just might equal more pay.

After reviewing your accomplishments with your boss, ask for suggestions to improve your format and revise it accordingly. Each year, save your accomplishment document. Collectively these documents represent your body of work. You'll need them when you update your résumé.

Accept feedback gracefully and gratefully. Don't expect to be told you're perfect, with nothing to work on. Such a review would be easy for your manager to give, but unhelpful to you. To get better and to understand your prospects, you want your manager to speak frankly. Let your manager talk while he's giving suggested areas of improvement. Don't interrupt to rebut what you're being told. Once it's your turn to talk, do so in a calm and non-defensive manner. If you haven't heard specifics about some aspect of your conduct that "could be improved," ask for examples. Write down the feedback so you can reflect on it after the meeting. While you may be tempted to ignore positive comments and focus on the negative ones, pay attention to the positives to continue identifying and building on your strengths.

NHL coach Mike Babcock offers this perspective: "When someone's got an issue with me, I like them to tell me so I can fix it and I can get better at it. And some people, when you give them feedback, they take that in a negative way. Whereas I think when people are trying to help you, that's a positive thing."

Work to change your behavior. Almost 60% of office workers say their reviews have "no impact on the way they approach their work." Be part of the minority who do something constructive with their evaluation—who listen, learn, and act on it. At appropriate times, ask for follow-up feedback to determine if you're improving in areas of concern.

3. Ensure Fair Compensation

If you own your own company, your employees are there to make you money. If you're employed by someone else, you're there to make other people money. Hopefully what you get in return—in additional to learning and gaining experience—is market pay. Schemes run the gamut from all salary and no bonus to little salary and mostly bonus, if earned.

Observe what your company does to discern its compensation philosophy. Good companies know what market compensation is for their people. Those with larger workforces often use a compensation consultant to examine industry data to determine how much people should be paid and how that pay should be structured between salary and bonus (and, if applicable, other forms of compensation). They establish a target percentile of what they want to pay in terms of total compensation versus the market, often between the 50th and 75th percentiles. Companies with smaller workforces may not have such a disciplined approach; they pay what they must to keep good people.

Good companies—large and small—maintain alignment in their pay practices such that they could post everyone's pay on the wall and defend it. When they hire, or try to retain someone who is threatening to leave, they are loyal to those who are already working at the company and not complaining. Pay throughout the organization is based on market pay and employee contribution. Those paid less might gripe about their pay, but their compensation is lower for a reason.

Whatever data, if any, your company uses, it's your manager's job to know market compensation for you, and to maneuver within the company to make sure you're paid appropriately. Likely your manager must keep your pay within company guidelines or argue persuasively why an exception should be made for you. It's possible that your manager knows you're underpaid but is unable to do anything about it. This is a problem for you both, but especially for you.

Companies have different compensation philosophies:

A bias toward high pay and high standards. The best companies know that the team with the best players usually wins and that the best players cost money. These companies are willing to pay close to or top dollar—maybe not at first, but once performance reveals who are the best performers. Standards are high, hours are long, and contribution is demanded. Aggressive types want to work at these companies, especially because performance bonuses often allow for out-sized compensation.

A bias toward low pay and high turnover. In these companies pay is within a narrow range based on position. Regardless of how good you are, other people have the same title as you, and your compensation is what employees with your title are paid. Pay increases are modest, and reluctantly given. Your compensation compared to industry peers is low. Accept it or leave.

A bias toward "cut your best deal" and lack of structure. At these places pay is low until people threaten to walk. Then managers may do what's necessary to "save" top contributors deemed worthy of saving. Unfairness is built into this compensation approach. It results in a widely varying pay "plan" that couldn't be defended if posted. It also penalizes loyalty and trust. This approach is used because it costs less and allows the owners to keep more of the pie.

> *As young professionals our slice of the compensation pie seems to be shrinking: on average we make 20% less than our parents did at the same age (adjusted for inflation). We've got a lot of advocating to do to catch up.*

Do any of these compensation plans fairly describe the approach at your company? Once you identify its philosophy, you can govern your behavior accordingly.

Discern your value. Having a reasonable approximation of your market-rate compensation allows you to be a more effective advocate for yourself when requesting a salary increase. Various sources are available at no cost to help you determine what you should be paid:

- Others in the organization who are doing work similar to yours
- Former colleagues who've left your company to take other jobs
- Contacts in your industry with jobs like yours
- Headhunters whom you've made part of your network
- Online databases such as the LinkedIn Salary Expectation Calculator, SAP SuccessFactors, Salary.com, PayScale.com, and others

You'll never know your true market value unless you get out there and see what you can get. Otherwise, the best you can do is to estimate a compensation range for people like you. Once you guesstimate that range, be satisfied if your pay is somewhere near the top. Don't sweat the discount.

Be careful when you seek higher compensation based on what a colleague allegedly makes. If you "look on someone else's plate," select a colleague who's a fair comparison in role and experience, and have your facts about his compensation right. Also, make sure your contribution is well regarded by your boss. You're inviting a comparison between your contribution and that of someone else, which is risky.

Make time for headhunters. Executive recruiters might be of service to help you determine your market value, assess your competencies, or even help you find a job. Often a headhunter will ask whether you know of anyone who might be interested in a position she is recruiting for, when really she is asking whether you might be interested. If so, play the game, recognizing that you can't be sure the caller is a headhunter. Get the job description and compensation facts. If asked directly whether you're interested, say you're happy in your present job and excited about your prospects. Keep the call brief or move the call to after-work hours. You're not doing anything inappropriate by getting a gauge of your market value.

If you ask for a raise, have a specific dollar amount in mind. Ask for an amount that ties to objective indications of your value. Don't expect your boss to propose a number. And be savvy about word choice. Don't say you "need" a raise. Who doesn't? Instead, demonstrate why you've "earned" a raise. Prepare for this discussion as you would for any difficult conversation (see "Lead"). Talk about your contribution, not about your personal life or expenses. Speak to your achievements clearly and cogently, and present any market data you have.

If you truly enjoy working at your company, convey your enthusiasm to your boss. Be specific—describe what you like about what you do and with whom you do it, including your boss. A request for more money will feel better to your boss if she knows that compensation is just one of the things about the job you value.

Understand your longer-term prospects. If your request for a pay increase is denied, or if the pay bump is less than you feel is justified, consider using this occasion to ask your boss to project the trajectory of your compensation over the next three to five years. Better to know than to toil on in ignorance, or hope. You might also ask for information about possible performance-based bonuses and, if your company has an LTIP (long-term incentive plan), how and when you might qualify.

Make exponential pay jumps. Starting from a low base salary and earning annual 3% cost-of-living bumps means you'll struggle to make a decent living. Which, in turn, means you'll struggle to get out of debt, buy a home,

start a family, pursue outside interests, see the world, help others; in other words, do things that matter to you. And you'll struggle to create investment income, which is taxed at lower rates than employment income. To live comfortably you're going to need some out-sized pay increases (10%, 15%, 20%) either by being promoted or by changing companies.

Transfer to the "in" department. Speaking of exponential pay jumps, in many companies there's a department or team that drives the business. In law it's the litigators; in real estate it's the developers; in medicine it's the surgeons. In Hollywood it's the A-listers. If there's an "in" department where you work, you already know which one it is. This department typically generates the most revenue, and hence it pays the most, and often launches the company's leaders, present and future. Those not in the group sometimes complain about those who are. "Why do they make more money?" Maybe even, "Why do they stay in better hotels?" If it's additional compensation you seek, and if your skill set fits, you could over time seek to transfer to this department. Often protocol dictates that you wait to be asked to join the "in" group, but you may prefer, instead, to take the initiative to advocate for yourself.

View yourself as an independent contractor. Always be growing your skill set to increase your desirability in the job market. Compensation is an important element of your job satisfaction. But so is doing work you like, with people you enjoy, in a city or town where you want to live. So, too, is amassing skills and knowledge in a field that's of great interest to you. If, considering pay and other factors, you can continue to pursue your career where you are now, that's terrific. If not, expect to change jobs from time to time to maximize your compensation. When you do, pay attention to the economic cycle. Often rising interest rates, increasing unemployment, stagnating wages, frothy real estate prices, and a run-away stock market suggest a recession may be coming soon. When it does, you'll want to be safely situated with gainful employment, not pounding a crowded pavement looking for a job at a time when few companies are hiring.

You and I must be prepared to change jobs—if not careers—multiple times during our working life. Employees between the ages of 21 and 38 are changing jobs three times more frequently than other workers. Sometimes this is due to "right-sizing," position elimination, or lack of fit. Other times we're not sufficiently challenged or feel we must move to get paid what we're worth. Whatever the reason for changing jobs, we need to possess the skills that allow us to make the transition smoothly and successfully.

Advocate for Others

Sometimes your advocacy concerns go beyond yourself. Advocate for those on your team, and for others at the company.

1. Defend

Rebut critical remarks. Advancement by members of your team is unlikely if those above you have a negative impression of them. When someone criticizes a member of your team with inaccurate or unfair remarks, set the record straight. You know your team and their performance best, and your silence in the face of criticism is implied agreement with that criticism. Speak up in order to correct misstatements of fact, put matters in context, or tell "the rest of the story." Neither you nor your team benefits from sniping by those outside it.

2. Shield

Be an umbrella. Your default mode is to be a team player who enthusiastically and consistently supports top-down goals, initiatives, and policies. You won't survive long if you fight your manager's initiatives, and those imposed on him from above. You'll soon be perceived as inflexible and an obstacle to progress if your standard reply is seen as "My answer is no; now, what is the question?" In good companies, most initiatives make sense and should be supported.

But not all. Some companies seemingly have a "fad of the month" that quickly fades. These initiatives consume much time and energy but soon fade. Some may, in your view, land poorly on your team or be a misguided use of people's time or company resources. Policies and established ways of doing things may have outlived their usefulness and need to be revised or simply eliminated. "Because we've always done it this way" isn't for you a compelling reason. Shield your team from rubbish flowing down from above.

The challenge is to be open to your manager's ideas and to new ways of doing things while, to the extent you can and always in appropriate ways, respectfully pushing back and shielding your team from things that are in your view flawed or ill-timed. One way to contribute is to offer a different perspective, perhaps one that's closer to the situation and prevents your boss from making a mistake (see "Contribute"). The ability to "speak truth to power" is a valuable skill, and another way to differentiate yourself. If you disagree with your manager about something of consequence, say so and offer an alternative solution. If you have the opportunity to speak before a decision is made, give your input. If not, as long as the matter remains undecided, speak promptly when you learn of it. Tread lightly if you take on pet peeves or matters im-

portant to your manager. Once the matter is decided, accept and support the decision.

> *When a fire that started at our under-construction apartment building destroyed houses across the street, my CEO decided we should provide free housing for displaced neighbors at one of our nearby communities. Seeing problems with this approach for my team, I advocated for other ways for us to provide free housing. I was given the chance to be heard, which is all one can ask. Once my view was rejected, I simply needed to execute the CEO's plan.*

Given the culture and personalities where you work, learn how and when to respectfully disagree, and when to let go of your objection. If you handle the conversation tactfully, good managers prefer and appreciate candid input to "yes-person" obedience. Have advocacy conversations with your manager in person, and privately, so you can judge the effect of your words and sense when to stop. Choose a good time, gather your facts, and proceed with tact, goodwill, and humor. Make sure you're viewed both as a team player and one who has your manager's—and the company's—best interests at heart.

3. Champion

Do more than defend and shield. Make sure your team members get the credit they deserve. Help them advance by championing them to those above. When you move to increase a team member's compensation or recommend her for promotion, those deciding must know her and appreciate her contribution. To prepare for that day now, speak well of your team members in conversations when they're not present and look for appropriate opportunities to "talk 'em up."

As a leader advocating for others, it's your job now to know market compensation to see that your team members are paid appropriately. If they're not, their substandard pay may become a problem for you. You'll have your own data points and anecdotal evidence, which may or may not be consistent with your company's plan. If you want to keep your team members, you'll need to fight for fair compensation for them, including what you believe are appropriate differences among pay. Some people are simply more valuable to your team and organization. And to you—perhaps because their skills complement yours. As such, they're more difficult to replace. From a business perspective, they're worth more and should be paid more. Know who these more valuable people are and why, and act accordingly. Although you won't

divulge your team member's compensation, people talk. You should be prepared to defend your pay scheme.

Promote carefully. Promoting top performers rewards them. It also reinforces your standards and strengthens your culture. Promoting the wrong people is more destructive than making a bad hire. Rewarding someone whose performance, or behavior, or character, is subpar sends a horrible message about your judgment and is demoralizing to the team. It weakens your standards and culture. Create a team whose members are a pleasure and privilege to champion.

Conclusion

It's fitting that we conclude our discussion of essential soft skills with "Advocate," since effective advocating for yourself and others relies on understanding the concepts and applying the skills previously covered in "Contribute," "Write," "Present," "Pitch," and "Lead." Advocacy at work starts with the strength of the relationships you build; the stronger the relationship between you and your manager, the more you can trust that the relationship will withstand your ask, whatever the outcome.

Without prompting, busy people, however well intentioned, will focus only so much on your needs and those of your team. So prompt them—judiciously and effectively. Your ability to defend, shield, and champion both yourself and your team members just might turn an unfulfilling job into one that holds great promise for you. Here's hoping!

Application: How to Leave

Despite advocating as best you can, you may decide—for lots of reasons—that you need to change jobs:

- To develop new skills
- To be paid what you're worth
- To escape a horrible boss
- To exit a toxic or low-pay work environment
- To depart ahead of being fired
- For personal reasons having nothing to do with your job

Warning signs of your impending termination include poor performance reviews, the expression of "concerns" about your ability to handle your job, flattening or even diminishing compensation (unrelated to a recession), repeated failure to be selected for desirable projects, and the marginalization of your team.

> *The relocation of your workspace to a storage closet in the basement is probably another sign that things aren't going so well.*

No matter what the reason for your departure, continue advocating for yourself as you leave. We send messages about who we are—and we advocate for ourselves—when we depart in a professional way. How you do so will be noticed by those where you worked and, if you have a new job, perhaps by those where you're heading.

It's not unusual to have done good work and still be let go. You may be leaving under circumstances that you perceive to be unfair. You may be angry. No matter. Your focus now is on your future, and it isn't on the place you're leaving. People leave jobs every day and thrive somewhere else. It's not unusual for people to say that leaving their prior place of employment, while hard at the time, was the best thing for their career. The odds are good that someday you'll say the same thing.

Time your departure. If self-selecting out, be thoughtful about when you give notice. Assume for planning purposes that when you do, you'll be asked to leave almost immediately. Absent some compelling reason, don't give notice in mid-December, when working two more weeks would've earned you an annual bonus. And don't give notice shortly before bonuses are paid—let

the check you worked so hard to earn clear the bank. Bigger picture, you may want to reach a certain level in your company before you leave. Or you may want to see a project through to strengthen your résumé.

Real estate guru Sam Zell, who started his law job on a Monday and quit that Friday at noon, says he practiced law "four and a half days too long." I made it longer than that, but despite working with people I enjoyed, I knew the work wasn't for me as I wanted to explore writing as a career.

Conversely, after deciding to change careers, I waited a whole year until I made partner before resigning from my law firm. I wanted that accomplishment on my résumé in case some day a retreat into law was required. Let your circumstances dictate the best time for you to give notice.

Give adequate notice. Offer to stay through the date required by company policy. If asked to stay longer and doing so doesn't create a conflict with your new employer, agree to a date that allows you to accomplish a project or something else of value to your current employer. If your employer doesn't want you to stay through the company's notice standard period, that's fine (and you assumed as much in your planning).

Stay focused and do your job through your last day. Don't coast to the finish line. Maintain full speed through your departure date. If you need a break, arrange for down time between jobs. Transition work and customer relationships as directed.

Don't take things without permission. We've talked about differentiating through character. Your departure is a moment when yours is on display. If you want something—documents, customer lists, product specifications, marketing materials, intellectual property—ask. Even if you created an item, it belongs to your employer if you created it during the time of your employment. Even if you believe an item is yours to take, don't do so without first discussing it with your manager. The company where you're going will have its own way of doing business. If it makes you feel better, materials taken tend to have less value—and for a shorter time—than people think.

Thank the right people for the opportunity they gave you. Whether you're being fired or leaving of your own volition, if you feel you've developed skills, gained knowledge, or met people who will aid you going forward, the gracious thing to do is to express your appreciation. Do so in person, then write a thank-you letter (not an email) after you leave. The letter—and the goodwill you create—may serve you well someday.

Ask for a recommendation, if warranted, regardless of company policy. Many large companies won't give a recommendation as a matter of policy; they will only confirm dates of employment. They fear being sued—by a former employee who claims to have been defamed by a bad recommendation, or by a company that alleges serious wrongdoing by a former employee who was hired on the basis of a good recommendation. Ask for a recommendation anyway. Don't ask someone in the HR department (unless you're in the HR department!). Ask someone who knows you and your work. If you're good enough, and your relationship is strong enough, this person may be willing to ask for and obtain permission . . . or just do it. No harm in asking. And, if you mean it, you might preface your request with, "I can hear no."

Mind your tongue, before and after departure. While still at your soon-to-be former job, disparage no one. Bad-mouthing people and engaging in passive-aggressive behavior will accomplish nothing but cause you regret later. If your employer hears of such behavior, expect to be putting your stuff in a box today. After you've left, continue to speak well of the company and the people you knew there. Disappoint those who call you wanting to hear bitterness and gossip.

When it's time to leave, go! What happens at your former place of employment no longer concerns you. Suppress your curiosity to see how they're managing without you. Even if you're interested in what's going on there, don't go back to visit. Long-term, maintain your contacts, but let time pass before connecting with former colleagues. If some are friends you want to lunch with, set boundaries. Don't talk shop about your former company—don't you bring it up, and, if your friend does, refuse to go there.

If your company offers you space on-site to work on your job search, decline it. Work from a coffee shop if you must, but get out. Don't be someone—or be perceived as someone—who clings to the past and can't move on. For your sake and theirs, separate physically and mentally.

Look Out Above!

Being fired is not unlike being dumped by your high school sweetheart. You cried, you pined for lost love, you tried numerous times to win her back, you wondered whom she was dating now, you talked about it with anyone who would listen. The next time a relationship ended, you'd learned how to behave and move on. Right?

Departing may be exciting if you're off to a new future of your choosing. Or it may be unpleasant and awkward, if you didn't choose. Either way, it will pass. Move on with dignity.

Question and Answer

1. How do I parlay a job offer into more money at my current job?

Carefully, if at all. No one likes to feel threatened, or to be given what they perceive to be an ultimatum. And some managers are offended that an employee would talk to a headhunter or consider leaving their company for any reason (even though they may not reciprocate the loyalty they require of you).

> *Dwight Schrute (of the American version of "The Office") has the right response to companies who don't walk their loyalty talk: "Would I ever leave this company? Look, I'm all about loyalty. In fact, I feel like part of what I'm being paid for here is my loyalty. But if there was somewhere else that valued loyalty more highly . . . I'm going wherever they value loyalty the most."*

It's risky to mention the other offer. If your company finds out about it on their own—and not because you talked about it—that's OK. The competing offer may be more powerful for you if you're not trying to use it as leverage. If you do disclose, don't use the other offer as a club. We've seen people disclose an offer as a tactic to get a pay raise and then be told—with "hearty" congratulations—they should take it and leave. Hard to say "never mind" after that.

If someone makes you an offer you think you cannot refuse, mull it over in private. Don't talk about it with your peers. If convinced you're underpaid, but want to stay, talk to your manager from a position of loyalty: "I really love the company, and I enjoy working with you, personally. I see myself here a long time." Then discuss your performance and the market data that suggests you are underpaid. If your pitch is unsuccessful, you may need to leave to be paid what you're worth.

2. The group I lead gets no respect. What can I do about it?

We talked earlier about transferring to the "in" department that drives the business, the one that seems to turn out future leaders. But the team you're leading isn't the "in" team. How do you increase its respect within the company and gain the rewards that go with such respect?

Earn more respect as a leader. Elevating your group internally starts with you. When you interact with peers who lead different groups, elevate the sta-

tus of your group by the force of your presence—by who you are and what you add to your peer group and company.

Add more value as a team. Changing perceptions requires sustained excellence and out-sized contributions by you and your team. That may mean bringing more to the company's bottom line, providing better support, or finding new ways to add value. Build a team whose results are too compelling to ignore.

Work well with other departments. Respond in a timely manner to their requests for information or help. When you need something from them, allow adequate time for them to comply. Do whatever you can to make it easier for them to provide it. If you're having a problem with another team, be diplomatic as you go about resolving it. Earn the reputation as a leader whose team is easy to do business with.

Change won't happen overnight, but you can elevate the status of your group. The "it" group can welcome others to the table. Who knows, someday someone from your group (maybe you) may sit at the company's inner table.

3. Any thoughts on championing myself in my résumé?

With the caveat that résumé writing is not the focus of *Look Out Above!*, we'll offer a few thoughts.

Your résumé introduces your writing skill. It will be judged on substance and style. It must also show what you can do as revealed by what you have done. Your writing must be correct, clear, and concise. To advocate for yourself in your résumé:

Keep it simple. Document your education, work history (in chronological order with the most recent job at the top), outside interests, and anything personal you choose to reveal. What more does anyone need to know?

Show your body of work. Make clear in your work history what you accomplished at each stop along the way. How did you add value? Can you fairly dollarize your contributions? Don't exaggerate your performance. Making unrealistic claims is a quick way to destroy trust and cast doubt on the accuracy of your résumé. Such exaggeration may also create doubt about what you say if you're interviewed.

Unless you burned a bridge, list in your work history the name and contact information of every person you reported to. A sharp interviewer will ask for it anyway (an interviewer like you—see "Lead"). Show by your transparency

that you had good rapport with each of your managers along the way. If your prior company has a policy of not discussing former employees, no matter. That's out of your control.

Emphasize your skills. After your work history, consider pulling together all the skills you've developed under a heading labeled "Skills." If you're trying to move from one industry to another where the applicability of your skills isn't as obvious, consider modifying the heading to say, "Transferable Skills." You're implying that the skills you've listed will ensure your effectiveness in a new role.

Avoid descriptions such as "Talented," "Driven to Succeed," "Goal-oriented," and "Motivated." These are unsupported claims, not skills. Examples of demonstrated skills include Analyzing Data, Leading Teams, Public Speaking, and Serving Customers. Even, if genuine, "Bringing Order to Chaos." A list of seven to ten skills works fine. Be ready to expand on every skill you claim.

Share outside interests. While some argue that employers don't care about a candidate's outside interests, we disagree. Outside interests reveal much about people, including their zest for life, sociability, and likability. Someone with interests and accomplishments outside of work—past and present—is more likely to be a lasting asset of the organization. That you were involved in scouting, played on your school's athletic teams, or were active in a large fraternity or sorority says something about your people skills. As does your current involvement in civic affairs or church work. Your résumé reader may be trying to determine whether you will mix well with clients. Outside interests provide an important clue.

Add a little humor to differentiate. If it comes naturally to you, use humor to show a touch of self-confidence and a sense of your style. Something subtle for you to laugh about with your interviewer, and that makes your résumé memorable.

The last item listed on my résumé was "Four-inch vertical leap and cat-like quickness." It never failed to get noticed or spark a discussion, in a good way.

4. Any Final Advocacy Tips and Tricks?

Beware your social media footprint. Your self-advocacy extends to the internet. A warning about what you post seems like such old news, but we know of people still blowing new opportunities or losing their jobs because of inappropriate content on their social media sites. Especially for those who lead and carry the responsibility of modeling, some content simply won't be tolerated. If you're not sure whether certain material is inappropriate, you have your answer. Don't post it.

Avoid opening a difficult negotiation with an apology. It sets a tone of weakness and may put you on the defensive from the outset, making it awkward for you to be assertive later. Save the opening apology for instances when one is truly required. Otherwise, you risk losing respect.

> *In a final attempt to salvage a real estate deal, my boss and I met with the person who had jacked us around on it. Since I had sourced the deal, I opened the meeting. As I heard myself begin by apologizing for something trivial, I suddenly realized I sounded like a schmuck. The look on my boss's face as I apologized confirmed that he agreed.*

Don't allow yourself to be intimidated into doing something you believe is wrong. Your advocacy skills may be required to extricate yourself from demands that violate your principles. Unlike the frog in the pot who doesn't jump out because the water is slowly turned to a boil, be mindful of what you're being asked to do and, over time, the kind of person you're becoming. Hopefully you won't be confronted with outrageous demands that give you little choice but to leave. Employees who, at the behest of their manager, lie to key stakeholders, or falsify earnings or test results, or engage in criminal acts, usually regret doing so. When exposed, their world comes crashing down.

> *When consulting, I interviewed a senior executive who commented, "This is the only place I've been where I've never been asked to do something wrong." A sad commentary on her prior employers.*

Develop mentors and sponsors. Seek the counsel of people more experienced who, having your best interests at heart, will guide and champion you. Look for people who'll get you unstuck when you're mired, see things you're missing, and help you devise your big-picture strategy. Such a relationship may shape your career, perhaps even change your life.

A mentor is someone you look to for encouragement, timely advice, wisdom, and, when needed, unfiltered truth ("your compensation is more than fair given your contribution") or a swift kick in the butt ("you need to do better work"). A mentor may also provide you with access to contacts. Over time you may find several mentors, both inside and outside your organization.

A sponsor could be a mentor, but, more narrowly, she is someone in your organization who advocates for you. She makes your presence known up the food chain, champions your advancement, and protects you from overhead cuts. The most likely candidate for this role is your manager, since she best knows your work. But if the time comes when your manager can no longer keep you on her team, a sponsor other than your manager may help you find a new position within the company.

> *Most mergers, acquisitions, and restructurings result in redundancy, and good people are let go. For you to keep your job during such times, sponsors are essential. You'll want someone to advocate for you with conviction when you're not present, especially as you progress higher up the corporate ladder.*

How do you "find" mentors and sponsors? We don't recommend asking someone directly to take on such a role. Although people do it, it's considered bad form. Usually such a relationship develops naturally over time between people who work together and become friends. As a potential mentee you must earn the relationship by first establishing yourself as a strong performer. And, to keep the relationship, follow the counsel you're given. Otherwise, mentors or sponsors will be reluctant to invest their time, talent, and possibly their reputation on your behalf.

If you don't want to wait for a relationship to develop, a more proactive approach is to ask questions of an appropriate person. Assuming that the result is a productive dialogue, you might ask permission to seek another question-and-answer session at some future time. To avoid being intrusive, pick your spots and frequency—and hope that an easy connection develops between you.

Like any friendship, mentor-and-sponsor relationships work best when mutually beneficial. While some people feel a need to "give back" by helping young people, others don't. So—in addition to your curious mind and sterling character—provide something of value to your mentors. Perhaps it will be your technology skills or help with social media or simply a young professional's perspective on things.

Replace lost mentors and sponsors. Over time you'll get promoted, and over time your mentors and sponsors will leave or retire. Once on your own you may feel a bit alone, even lonely, in a changing world. Keep cultivating new folks to guide and support you. And, as you progress, consider reversing roles by mentoring some young professionals whose aspirations, ability, and work ethic are compatible with your own.

Transform!

CHAPTER SEVEN

"I think in life you should work on yourself until the day you die."

SERENA WILLIAMS, TENNIS PRO, ACTIVIST

Transform

Now that you've expanded the scope of what you can do, let's explore what you can become.

Over the course of our lives we search for many things. For a way to support ourselves, and provide food, clothing, and shelter. For companionship, romance, and love. For fun, adventure, and physical challenge. For meaning, happiness, and success, however we define those terms. We search—at different times with different intensity—for all that matters to us.

There are many parallels between our search for a satisfying worklife and the quest archetype so prevalent in books, movies, and gaming. In genres as diverse as epic poetry (Homer's *The Odyssey*), literature (L. Frank Baum's *The Wizard of Oz* and Tolkien's *The Lord of the Rings*), and film (George Lucas' *Star Wars*), a heroic quest has certain basic elements: a hero, a perilous journey that ends in a crucial struggle between the hero and an evil foe, and the hero's triumphant return. Ultimately, the significance of a successful quest is the personal transformation of the hero.

In one archetypal form of the quest, a youthful hero embarks on a journey. She doesn't yet know what she's capable of, and she lacks experience in the ways of the world. She soon finds herself in an unfamiliar land of danger and opportunity. She may have guides (gods, humans, animals, *Look Out Above!*) on the journey that give advice or provide some magical item (sword, sandals, light saber, *Look Out Above!*) that helps her succeed. Over the course of her quest she discovers that she possesses qualities that make her heroic:

7

- Audacity, courage, grit, and a willingness to sacrifice for a higher cause
- Strength to defend, and the skill to wield some weapon effectively
- Common sense, wits, and the wisdom to strategize, follow advice, and distrust appearances

This combination of survival traits allows the youthful hero to improvise and adapt as the situation requires and, after great hardship, succeed.

A few of my favorite quest narratives are Robert Louis Stevenson's Treasure Island, Indiana Jones and the Last Crusade, *the Cream song* "Tales of Brave Ulysses," *and, as an example of the "inner quest," J. D. Salinger's* The Catcher in the Rye. *What are yours?*

As the protagonist in your quest for worklife success, you too will face external obstacles. Not the Cyclops, a wicked witch, or Darth Vader, but perhaps their modern version—a horrible boss, a disingenuous colleague, or tough competitors both inside and outside your company. More likely, you'll encounter gatekeepers who block your path because, in their view, you're under-qualified, or over-qualified, or not the right fit, or too young, or too old. You'll also encounter people who don't do what they say they will do, or who are unresponsive to your calls, texts, emails, or proposals. And maybe a few who never acknowledge—much less reciprocate—a favor or kindness done.

You'll be placed in situations where you must perform before you think you're ready. You may need training that isn't provided, forcing you to learn on your own and improvise as you go. You may have to meet expectations you weren't informed about or aware of. You may face unwanted sexual advances. You may be passed over, underpaid, and perhaps let go, with or without regard to performance. You may do excellent work, but your company may fail.

Just as daunting are the internal obstacles—self-doubt, fear, and laziness. It's not easy to make yourself show up day after day and do your best work, to muster the self-discipline to pursue skills and knowledge on your own time, and, if necessary, to start a new course while financial realities press you to remain on the path you're on. Your journey is indeed difficult, which makes your story interesting and a successful outcome so satisfying.

Most quest stories conclude with the hero returning home to live, presum-ably, happily ever after. Odysseus returns to Ithaka, vanquishes a pack of suitors, and reunites with Penelope. After three clicks of her shoes, Dorothy makes it back to Kansas. Indiana Jones returns to teach at Marshall College.

Your quest, however, has no such predictable ending. Finding your niche, executing your life's work, and contributing to the greater good will probably last most of your life. You'll move from one position or opportunity to another, and continually reinvent yourself as you better discover who you are and what you want to do next. You're engaged in a lifelong process of growing, changing, and becoming.

Like all questing heroes, you're strengthened by the process of struggling to achieve goals, emerging more resilient and worldly-wise. While it's satisfying to have something tangible to show for your work (like a nice salary, a car that you enjoy, or a home that you own—perhaps even some net worth), your inner transformation is the real story, the prize to be won. You're not the same because your confidence in what you can do—and what you think you can do—has expanded. You may even come to realize that no matter what happens to you in the working world, you will adjust, survive, and ultimately thrive.

And so, we conclude *Look Out Above!* with the transformation process, which we believe transcends the importance of any job.

What Do You Seek?

Let's start big-picture. What do you want out of your work? Think about what worklife success looks like for you. To stimulate your thinking, we offer this definition of worklife success:

> *I'm achieving worklife success when I am becoming good at something I enjoy doing, in an environment I enjoy, for the benefit of myself and others.*

Success means feeling good about where you are. Even if you see your current job as part of a grander plan, you're where you want to be, at least for now. You're excited about what you're doing, where you're doing it, and with whom. You're learning new things and being challenged. As *Breaking Bad*'s Walter "Heisenberg" White explained to his wife when revealing what kept him in the drug business: "I liked it. I was good at it. And I was really . . . I was alive." You, too, feel awake, alert, and alive (hopefully doing something else!).

Success means developing expertise at something. Which, of course, takes time. As Justice Oliver Wendell Holmes said, "The great thing in this world is not so much where we are but in what direction we are moving." Hopefully you like the progress you're making, and are receiving positive recognition for your contribution. It's a good feeling to receive compliments on your work and to have your ideas taken seriously.

Success is about yourself and about others. Early in your career you're not as likely to be concerned about others as you are about becoming self-supporting and finding work you enjoy. You'll want to generate enough income to support yourself without relying on anyone and, if necessary, to get out of debt. Ultimately, however, as you progress you may be unsatisfied if you don't create some benefit beyond yourself. If you feel that way, maybe you'll choose work that benefits others, or that provides you the financial resources to do so. Perhaps you'll satisfy this need by doing something outside work.

So, what is *your* definition of success, at least for now? Your vision could be as simple as making a certain amount of money every year. Or using specific skills that you enjoy using and want to develop further. It could be creating your own business, or working a job that allows you to develop the skills and knowledge to later be your own boss. Your vision could be to work a set number of hours, or to work outdoors, or from home. Maybe you want to live near family and friends, or in a certain city with a stimulating culture and nightlife. Your vision of a successful worklife will involve multiple items, and their combination will be uniquely yours.

Now, get specific. However you define success, and whatever it is you decide to seek, describe it to yourself as clearly as possible and probe why it's what you want to pursue. Write down your thoughts. Considering specifics will help you sharpen your vision as you gravitate to the opportunities, people, and resources you seek. It will also help you prioritize what is and isn't important, and spur you on when motivation flags. Discontent with where you are may be a signal that you're off course in realizing your vision and need to reset.

An intense desire to achieve something for a purpose you value deeply, and can articulate, trumps a wouldn't-it-be-nice-if dream. In times of discontent and discouragement, which you can count on, knowing and reaffirming your "why" may provide the motivation to keep going. If you can't find a "why" that resonates, question whether this vision or goal has sufficient meaning for you to be achieved. A "why" that has meaning should strongly propel you.

A friend who hiked the entire Appalachian Trail (about 2,200 miles) tells of meeting and talking to lots of hikers along the way. Most, he said, never achieved their stated goal of hiking from Georgia to Maine. He believed they quit because "they never knew why they were there in the first place." He went to rethink his life and priorities, to have an adventure, and to seek a deeper spiritual connection. He didn't come back until he found what he was after.

What Will Be Required

Now that you've clarified what it is you seek, what will it take to get it? Looking to the quest genre for guidance, certain elements seem essential to the successful achievement of any quest, be it to slay the dragon, free people from tyranny, or achieve desired worklife success. As you go forth to challenge yourself and the world:

Believe. Your success will start—or stop—here. A deep-rooted belief in yourself will have a tremendous impact on your outcome. While we're all a work in progress, you believe in your ability, judgment, and equal right with others to achieve and enjoy success. You believe that you can make it in this world, and that no matter what the challenge you will, ultimately, figure out a way through. Yours isn't a rose-colored view of yourself, but a comfort level with who you are and what you're in the process of becoming. Of course self-doubt appears from time to time, but it's not so deep-rooted that it prevents you from getting what you want out of life.

To the greatest extent that you can, believe in yourself—that you can, and will, succeed. Be optimistic about your life and your prospects. Notice personal victories, large and small, that give credence to your belief. Believe that something good will come from your endeavors, even if the good may differ from what you envision.

Your self-belief will manifest itself in confidence. Perhaps no trait is more indicative that an inner transformation is taking place than confidence. How we carry ourselves affects how others see us and how we see ourselves. Confident people are comfortable with who they are. They aren't riddled with fear about failing, which they realize is part of the growth process. They aren't overly concerned with what people think. Confidence allows them to take risks, to ask questions, to appear silly. This confidence is attractive and attracts good things.

The judge I clerked for was once accosted by a lawyer who criticized the judge for an opinion he had written. To hear the lawyer tell it, the opinion was flawed in every way—it failed to follow prior case law, created dangerous precedent, and damaged his client. After listening politely, the judge replied, "You know, I didn't write it with you in mind." The judge's point is instructive. Not everything we offer, or say or do, will resonate with everyone. It would be unreasonable to expect otherwise. Seek to master your craft and do your best work. And, undaunted, keep believing in yourself: don't be dissuaded or discouraged by the inevitable critics.

Help yourself succeed by choosing to be confident. Make confidence in your-self a reality by acting as if you already have it. The alternative—waiting until you achieve success, then hoping your success gives you confidence—seems unlikely. Even if you don't feel it, present yourself with confidence. Most people will step aside to let someone pass who acts as if he knows what he's doing. When you catch yourself imagining failure, flip your mental switch to imagine success. Take inventory of your strengths and the good things in your life. Recall and build on past moments when you succeeded, and on what others say they like and admire about you.

Confidence is one of the things—maybe even "the" thing—we lack as young professionals. Look Out Above*! is intended to help readers transition from uncertain to confident employees. Ultimately, worklife confidence will come from confronting challenges, gaining experience, and achieving success. Until then, we must seem rather than be.*

Believing in yourself will require easing up on the self-criticism. When get-ting down on yourself, engage in positive self-talk, then move the mental conversation from what happened (past tense) to what you're going to do next (future tense). Regrets about yesterday's decisions, actions, inactions, and results can block us from moving forward. Wishing we'd done better in school, earned a graduate degree, taken a certain job, had a different boss, or given a better presentation isn't productive. So, too, with wishing that we had made better use of time gone by. Everyone has regrets. Use yours as mo-tivation to move on and do better. As the sage says, "The second-best time to plant a tree is today."

Risk. Questing heroes take up the challenge. They leave the comfort of their physical and emotional surroundings to set forth on a journey. They may be reluctant, but they overcome their fear, self-doubt, and the paralysis of analysis—and they go. They are willing to trade a safe life for the unknown.

Accepting risk speeds the learning process. Those who put themselves in chal-lenging situations discover more quickly what works—and what doesn't—and how to adapt. They gain confidence as they realize their capabilities are greater than they thought. Whether it's giving a presentation, making an idea pitch, cold-calling prospects, launching a product, or starting a com-pany, those who risk are moving up the learning curve. Sometimes the great-est risk is doing nothing.

For you, risk may mean taking on new challenges such as initiating a diffi-cult conversation, starting a project, or volunteering for an assignment whose

details are sketchy. After several years of worklife experience, it may involve stepping into a leadership role in your company or leaving to begin a new job, perhaps in another city.

> *With my third child on the way, I quit my law partnership, took a 50% cut in pay, and started at the bottom of a real estate development firm in another city. Encouraged by a supportive spouse, it was the best career move I ever made.*

So be bold and take some risks. A Latin proverb says, "Fortune favors the bold, but abandons the timid." William James advised: "To change one's life: (1) Start immediately, (2) Do it flamboyantly, (3) No exceptions." Take some risks with your work—both what you do and how you do it. Create a body of work and network of relationships that you're proud of. Here's wishing each of us the courage to live life a little bolder every day, starting with our work.

> *Every year across the nation terrified first-year law students are called upon at random to stand, recite the facts of the assigned case, and then be intellectually disemboweled by the professor. Years ago, at the University of Virginia School of Law, after being called on one student stood and replied, "I am [name redacted] of the Law Review, and if I have something to say I will raise my hand and say it." Then he sat down, to stunned silence. His audacity became the stuff of legend. This student later served as dean of the law school!*

Be thoughtful about when to say "no," and when to say "yes." You won't accomplish much if you say "yes" to every opportunity and request. Maintaining your focus is key to realizing your goals and achieving what matters most to you. If you dilute your time and talent by taking on too much, you'll likely succeed at very little and disappoint others and yourself. Saying "no"— cheerfully and definitively—allows you to focus on high-leverage activities.

But if you never say "yes" to new challenges, you'll never realize the benefits of growth that follow. Experience can't turn into wisdom without the experience. Nothing much happens to people who always find a reason to say "no." Opportunities are rarely perfect. There's always something that could be better, or more certain, that makes leaping a tough call. If you require perfection—or a sure thing—you'll never risk. Do your analysis and trust

your instinct. And if you say "yes," get going. As Dr. Martin Luther King Jr. observed, "We are confronted with the fierce urgency of now . . . there is such a thing as being too late. Procrastination is still the thief of time. Life often leaves us standing bare, naked, and dejected with a lost opportunity."

Persevere. Heroic questors are tough. They demonstrate bulldog-like grit, pluck, resolve. They don't give up, no matter how difficult the task. For you, persevering will mean learning new skills, and that means being bad before you're good. Maintaining your resolve requires both effort and suffering as you stick with something hard when you want to quit.

Expect your quest to be difficult. Life is difficult; work is difficult. Lots of people may want what you want. Creating a worklife in synch with your vision—both big-picture and more specific—isn't easy. Recognizing this reality may help you resist looking for shortcuts that aren't there and overcome the temptation to give up. Keep pushing yourself.

Expect some failures. Everybody fails, especially those who take risks. Successful questors get up and keep going. Winston Churchill defined success as "going from failure to failure without loss of enthusiasm." Failure moves you closer to success if you learn from it. One success—after repeated failures—can launch or make your career.

Losses are more instructive than victories. True professionals— at anything—know the importance of failure, and how to use it constructively. They use failure to focus their improvement. They analyze what went wrong and identify the skills and strategies they must improve to succeed.

Don't worry if you can't envision now all the steps required for success. You can't know all the challenges that will arise, much less how you will address them. Go as far as you can. Trust that when you get there, you'll see how to go farther and that doors will open as you progress.

Adapt. Persevering is toughing it out. Adapting is doing something different when what you're doing isn't working. It's not merely plowing forward, but going forward with a new plan. As Mike Tyson said, "Everyone has a plan until they get punched in the face." Heroic questors often find that strength alone is inadequate to defeat the enemy. They don't just get up and dust off when knocked down; they learn from adversity and, deploying wits and cunning, they revise their plan. The goal—and their determination to achieve it—doesn't change. But their approach does.

For you in the workplace, adapting may mean trying to find new ways to please a demanding client who, dissatisfied with your work, is pushing you to be better. It may mean taking tough performance feedback from your boss to heart and doing something about it. It may require giving yourself time to catch up when colleagues seem more confident and skilled than you. Or finding workarounds when your preferred way forward is to be chosen or hired by someone else, and they don't oblige.

Look first at yourself. If you don't get the desired response from your written report or presentation, or if your idea isn't approved, or you don't get the promotion you believe you deserve, how will you react? Start with the assumption that maybe you're the problem. Do some introspection about what you're doing that may be counter-productive. Consider asking a trusted friend for feedback about your approach. Then decide what must change. This may mean, for some, getting up earlier, setting aside focus time, or breaking down large projects into small ones if that helps you start and not procrastinate.

As you adapt and develop new plans, be thoughtful about your choices. You know by now that choices bring consequences, including choices not to act or risk. Our choices are reflected in our words and actions—how we approach a given situation, respond to adversity, and choose our circle of friends and associates. Some choices we must continually make: "What activities are worth my time?" "What's the best use of my time right now?" "How much time is a given activity worth?" Just because we can do something—and do it well—doesn't mean it's worth doing. Without thought and intentional direction, years seem to just "happen," flowing by as if of their own volition.

Bad choices, once made, can sometimes be reversed. Perhaps you said "yes" to something when in hindsight you should have said "no," or you allowed someone to make a choice for you that you now regret. Or you've invested time, resources, and emotional energy into something you now think was— and is—a mistake. Sunk costs are, by definition, sunk. To reassess a bad choice, try to project its short- and long-term outcomes. Determine if it's smart to continue investing in, say, a project or opportunity or relationship— or if it's time to get out. Think carefully about how to extract yourself if you decide to reverse course. Doing so often requires you to have a difficult conversation.

Sometimes we tell ourselves and others that we have "no choice." While this unfortunate reality may sometimes be true, make it a practice to challenge this assumption. Even if none of the alternatives you see before you seem feasible, the projected outcome may be so unacceptable that you'll be forced to try something. Options are almost always there; they may be limited— certainly not ideal—but with work one may emerge you can live with.

A former boss was big on optionality. To tell him he "had no choice" was to incur certain push-back. He insisted on having options so as not to be maneuvered into a corner where someone dictated what he had to do. In the business world, having no choice leads to bad outcomes.

Get help. Be willing to ask for help whenever you need it. And take help from wherever you can find it. Greek and Roman stories are full of questing figures who sought aid from powerful rulers or direction from wise mentors (remember the Oracle at Delphi?). Expose yourself to knowledgeable people in fields that interest you. Find a mentor or two to guide you and hold you accountable. Friends too are a big part of our world. Choose some whose talent you admire and who, because they expect you to make the most of your talents, push you to be better. Share your goals and aspirations with a few friends you trust. Ideally, your close circle of friends will be people you can learn from and who will learn from you.

Give help. When questing heroes succeed in their quest, they benefit the lives of others and help those in need as they go. Those in the village are liberated when the dragon is slain or when the tyrant is vanquished and the rightful kingdom is restored. Give back as you go. Use some of your time and talent to encourage, teach, and coach others. Speak well of people, and when you see them perform well in their job, congratulate them. Write letters on their behalf. What we intend to do doesn't count; it's what we do that matters.

When I was a young attorney, I conducted a difficult deposition on my own in a distant city with an experienced attorney representing the other side. Afterward, he wrote a letter to my senior partner saying nice things about my performance and potential. I've never forgotten this gesture. So too, unexpected gestures that you do for people will be appreciated and long remembered.

Parting Thought

To become a better employee, team member, writer, presenter, leader, *anything*, you'll need to grow. One year from now, you'll be the same person you are now unless you meet new people, try new things, have new experiences, develop new skills, or learn more about the things that impact your world. Like heroic questors, you'll need to muster the courage to move out of your

comfort zone and pay the price in terms of time, effort, and opportunities you forego.

A leading executive recruiter advises: "We look for candidates who have intellectual curiosity. They might be voracious readers, work with executive coaches, attend conferences, take classes, surround themselves with stimulating people, travel, etc. However they do it, they realize they don't know it all and they work to expand their knowledge base. And thereby separate themselves from the field." In the next few months, how and where will you meet new people? What new experiences do you intend to have? What skills and knowledge do you intend to acquire? How will you do so?

German composer and organist Johann Pachelbel (1653–1706) served as the organist for the Protestant church in Erfurt. His job description required that every year on St. John the Baptist Day (June 24), he was to observe the anniversary of his employment by submitting to a re-examination recital to demonstrate his vocational progress during the prior year. What if every year each of us had to submit to an exam to show our progress? Much like an annual review, but broader. Applying this concept to your life, what would you do to prepare for such an exam? Would you be happy with the result?

Often people who seek deeper knowledge of a specific field already know something about their subject. People who read books about art already have some knowledge and love of art; people who read financial blogs invest; and people who study tennis technique online can already keep the ball in play. So, too, those reading a book about PowerPoint can already create a slide. We think there's a simple reason why those past the beginner stage are the ones who seek a deeper understanding of how to progress further. Having achieved some success, they realize they have much to learn and have a strong desire to grow and be better still.

We suspect this describes you. We hope you find *Look Out Above!* to be of value in accelerating your growth process. We hope too that your journey, with its ongoing challenges, will be exhilarating and full of rewards. May it continue for the rest of your life!

Good luck to us all.

Best, Bob and Nick

Ithaka

by C. P. Cavafy, translated by Edmund Keeley
and Philip Sherrard

When you set out for Ithaka
pray that your road's a long one,
full of adventure, full of discovery.
Laistrygonians, Cyclops,
angry Poseidon—don't be scared of them:
you won't find things like that on your way
as long as your thoughts are exalted,
as long as a rare excitement
stirs your spirit and your body.
Laistrygonians, Cyclops,
wild Poseidon—you won't encounter them
unless you bring them along inside you,
unless your soul raises them up in front of you.

Pray that your road's a long one.
May there be many a summer morning when—
full of gratitude, full of joy—
you come into harbors seen for the first time;
may you stop at Phoenician trading centers
and buy fine things,
mother of pearl and coral, amber and ebony,
sensual perfumes of every kind,
as many sensual perfumes as you can;
may you visit numerous Egyptian cities
to fill yourself with learning from the wise.

Keep Ithaka always in mind.
Arriving there is what you're destined for.
But don't hurry the journey at all.
Better if it goes on for years
so you're old by the time you reach the island,
wealthy with all you've gained on the way,
not expecting Ithaka to make you rich.

Ithaka gave you the marvelous journey.
Without her you wouldn't have set out.
She hasn't anything else to give.

And if you find her poor, Ithaka won't have fooled you.
Wise as you'll have become, and so experienced,
you'll have understood by then what an Ithaka means.

Notes and Sources

What follows should lead you to what you want and provide proper attribution to those whose research and quotes lent a much-needed air of dignity to *Look Out Above!*

Start Here

1 *Opening quote.* Born in 1799, Amos Bronson Alcott was an American teacher and writer. He was an abolitionist, an advocate for women's rights, and a "vegan" before anyone knew what that was. His daughter Louisa May wrote *Little Women.*

3 *Academic success has a short shelf life in the working world.* "Nobody cares about your GPA outside of college. If you earned a 4.0, then you wasted your time. My GPA was a 0.3, and I own a toaster that can toast four pieces of bread at once." Article by Paul Ryan in the *Duluth Reader*, "Stupid Advice for Naive Graduates," May 31, 2012.

6 *Soft skills and people skills account for 85% of success in business.* So says the National Soft Skills Association (and they should know!), which in turn cites research conducted by Harvard University, the Carnegie Foundation, and Stanford Research Center. Soft skills, also known as transferable or professional skills, include communication, critical thinking, and teamwork skills. The remaining 15% of job success is attributed to hard skills—technical skills and knowledge.

6 *Study of almost 8,000 college-educated millennials.* From *The 2016 Deloitte Millennial Survey.* Deloitte surveyed nearly 7,700 Millennials from 29 countries. All participants had a college or university degree

and were employed full-time. Most worked in the private sector in large companies (over 100 people).

6 *Most people read zero business books each year.* So says master marketer and author Seth Godin in a blog post, *Fully Baked*, September 29, 2016. But successful people—like you—read business books. Bill Gates reads fifty books a year. Warren Buffet reads five hundred pages a day. Mark Zuckerberg started a book club to challenge himself to read a book every two weeks. One study shows that 88% of wealthy respondents read at least thirty minutes a day, and 63% listen to audio books as they commute. See article by Carrie King, Blinkist.com Magazine Posts, April 20, 2018.

6 *Employers are demanding more, sooner.* From an article by Lauren Weber and Chip Cutter in the *Wall Street Journal*, "A Wake-Up Call for Grads: Entry-Level Jobs Aren't So Entry Level Any More," May 10, 2019.

7 *Ignatius J. Reilly.* From John Kennedy Toole, *A Confederacy of Dunces*, Louisiana State University Press, 1980. Now considered a classic of twentieth-century Southern literature, Toole's work was awarded the Pulitzer Prize for Fiction in 1981. Due to the persistent efforts of his mother, who brought his manuscript to one publisher after another, the book was published eleven years after Toole's death.

Chapter 1: Contribute

9 *Opening quote.* Beryl Markham quote from her book *West into the Night*, reprint by North Pointe Press, 1983 (book originally published in 1942). Markham is recalling advice given to her by her father.

11 *"Individual acts of perversion so profound and disgusting."* From the Statement of Charges against the Delta Tau Chi Fraternity read by Douglas C. Neidermeyer, sergeant-at-arms, in *Animal House*, Paramount Pictures, 1985.

13 *Commitment requires more than mere intention.* For an article on the meaning of commitment, and on the relationship between stated intention (easy) and a willingness to do what it takes to make that intention a reality (hard), see Mel Schwartz writing in *Psychology Today*, "What do we mean by commitment?," October 28, 2009.

14 *Two-thirds of employees are "Not Engaged" or "Actively Disengaged" at work.* From a Gallup.com poll, as reported by Amy Adkins, 2014. Millennials were the least engaged group at 28.9%.

28 *Aristotle's principle of habituation.* Ancient Greek philosopher and scholar Aristotle tutored Alexander the Great and set up a school of rhetoric called the Lyceum.

29 *Avoid the appearance of impropriety.* See Canon 2 of the Model Code of Judicial Conduct. A similar canon used to apply to lawyers, but was dropped!

30 *Create a favorable first impression.* Knowing how to shake hands must be a lost art, as companies are hiring consultants to teach young professionals to do just that (some don't know the look-people-in-the-eye part). From an article by Kate King in the *Wall Street Journal*, "Wanted: Employees Who Can Shake Hands, Make Small Talk," December 9, 2018.

31 *We're not a family, but a high-performing team.* Robert Lane quote from an article by Ilan Brat and Timothy Aeppel in the *Wall Street Journal*, "Why Deere Is Weeding Out Dealers Even as Farms Boom," published August 14, 2007.

32 *Millionaires "most important" and "least important" success factors.* From Thomas J. Stanley, *The Millionaire Mind*, Andrews McMeel Publishing, 2002.

36 *Most people fail because they don't understand their business.* Carl Sewell introduced innovations at his Cadillac dealership in Dallas that are now adopted throughout the industry. People came to Dallas to tour his dealership and learn his techniques. Sewell was the first to offer loaner cars, and to install a cafeteria, playroom, and interior glass windows so customers could see the work area where mechanics worked on their cars. Quote taken from his book, *Customers for Life: How to Turn That One Time Buyer into a Lifelong Customer*, Pocket Publishing, 1998.

36 *McDonald's is in the real estate business.* Ray Kroc quote oft-cited; supposedly from his remarks to an MBA class at the University of Texas at Austin in 1974.

36 *Rolex is in the luxury business.* Andre Heiniger quote from Mark McCormack, *What They Don't Teach You at Harvard Business School*, Bantam, 1984.

42 *Study showing that people don't ask for help or advice to avoid looking incompetent.* From an article by Joseph Steinberg in *Fortune*, "This Bad Habit Could Be Holding You Back at Work," November 15, 2015.

43 *Pareto Principle.* Named after economist Vilfredo Pareto, this principle holds that roughly 80% of effects come from 20% of causes. It suggests, then, that much of what we do every day is pointless!

Chapter 2: Write

45 *Opening quote.* Hemingway quote from Arnold Samuelson, *With Hemingway*, 1984.

47 *Survey of 120 major American corporations finding that writing is a "threshold skill" for salaried employees.* Report of the College Board's National Commission on Writing, "Writing: A Ticket to Work . . . Or a Ticket Out," A Survey of Business Leaders, September 2004.

47 *"Written Communications" skill is "very important" to 93.1% of employers.* From a study of over four hundred U.S. employers conducted by the Conference Board, the Partnership for 21st Century Skills, Corporate Voices for Working Families, and the Society for Human Resource Management, *Are They Really Ready to Work?*, 2006.

47 *Peter Drucker.* Quote widely available. Drucker was a management consultant and author who has been described as the founder of modern management.

48 *English majors are increasingly favored in the hiring process.* From an article by Kaleigh Moore on Inc.com, "Study: 73% of Employers Want Candidates with this Skill," April 7, 2016.

48 *College Board study concluding that one-third of employees do not meet the writing requirements of their jobs.* From the Associated Press as reported on MSNBC.com, "Survey Shows Workers Shud [*sic*] Write Better," September 9, 2004.

48 *Why so many employees don't meet the writing requirements of their job.* Quote by Manpower EVP Bram Lowsky, as reported in an article on MSNBC.com by Kelley Holland, "Why Johnny Can't Write, and Why Employers Are Mad," November 11, 2013.

51 *Write newspaper—and not magazine—style.* Paul Tudor Jones quote from an article by Sarah Grant on Bloomberg.com, "Billionaire Paul Tudor Jones to Staff: Learn to Write or I'll Rip Up Your Memo," October 23, 2015.

59 *There is only great rewriting.* Louis Brandeis was a Supreme Court Justice. Similar is novelist Nathaniel Hawthorne's observation: "Easy reading is damn hard writing."

59 *Editing to remove dangling snippets of a line (however OCD!).* Why then, you may ask, does *Look Out Above!* contain some dangling line snippets? Because we can't know when writing what the final page layout will look like.

65 *It's never been easier to find a synonym or check your grammar usage.* Current sources include thesaurus.com, merriam-webster.com, wordhippo.com, quickanddirtytips.com, and grammarly.com.

67 *Hemingway's writing never sent anyone to a dictionary.* According to *Quote Investigator*, Faulkner's quote about Hemingway was from an address to a creative writing class at the University of Mississippi in April 1947; the text wasn't published until the summer 1951 issue of the *Western Review*.

67 *Study showing people who write using complicated words are perceived as less intelligent by readers.* From an article by Sue Shellenbarger in the *Wall Street Journal*, "How to Look Smarter," January 16, 2015.

68 *Vocabulary words:* Shakespeare 21,000, average person at time of Shakespeare 700. From Jay Heinrich, *Thank You for Arguing*, Three Rivers Press, 2007. Depending how you count words, the average person today knows around 40,000 words. The point isn't one's absolute number count, but relative count and ability to clearly articulate concepts vis-à-vis peers.

68 *Study showing that college students who scored in the top 5% on the vocabulary test later earned the highest incomes.* From Earl Nightingale, *Lead the Field*, chapter 10, "One Thing You Can't Hide," Nightingale-Conant Corporation, 1968.

72 *Don't "Reply All" to an email about your meeting availability.* Better still, if it's you organizing the meeting, use a shared calendar app. As you probably know, such an app allows participants to view, schedule, and update events on a "shared" calendar without back-and-forth emails and time wasted. Bigger picture, look for technology tools and tips of every sort to increase your efficiency and to allow you more time and energy to focus on creating work that differentiates you. If need be, find a techie to tutor you.

73 *Ill-advised email about design drawings.* Email from Korea Brass representative to Lionel LLC's director of engineering, as reported in Todd Sawicki's article, "Details of the MTH vs. Lionel Verdict," *O-Gauge Railroading*, December 2004.

73 *Ill-advised email written by NFL trainer.* From an article by Rick Maese in the *Washington Post*, "NFL Abuse of Painkillers and Other Drugs Described in Court Filings," March 9, 2017.

73 *GM list about words not to be used.* From an article by Sam Frizell in *Time*, "These Are the 69 Words GM Employees Were Forbidden from Using," May 14, 2014. See also an article in the *Detroit Free Press* by Brent Snavely and Alisa Priddle, "GM's Banned Words: What's Wrong with Using Plain English?," June 17, 2014.

77 *"Dash but don't be rash."* From Mark Davidson, *Right, Wrong, and Risky*, W. W. Norton (2006). If you want a readable grammar book with a sense of humor, this is your book.

Chapter 3: Present

79 *Opening quote.* Millennials were fortunate to grow up reading *Calvin and Hobbes*, arguably the greatest comic strip of all time. Creator Bill Watterson offered gentle but profound wisdom about life and human nature through the eyes of a first-grader, Calvin, and his stuffed animal best friend Hobbes. Perhaps you recall Susie Derkins, Mrs. Wormwood, Spaceman Spiff, Stupendous Man, Deranged Mutant Killer Monster Snow Goons, the Transmogrifier, and the top-secret G.R.O.S.S. (Get Rid Of Slimy girlS) club. Watterson's 1991 commencement speech at his alma mater Kenyon College is terrific. Find it by searching Kenyon College Commencement: May 20, 1990.

81 *Some 35m PowerPoint presentations are given every day.* From Poll Everywhere blog, "Stories, Tips, and New Features from the People of Poll Everywhere." Poll Everywhere blog also source for fact that average slide contains forty words.

81 *Over four hundred U.S. employers say "Oral Communications" skill is the most important business skill.* From a study conducted by The Conference Board, the Partnership for 21st Century Skills, Corporate Voices for Working Families, and the Society for Human Resource Management, *Are They Really Ready to Work?*, 2006.

81 *In a study of company directors, 63% believe that presentation skills are more important for career success than intelligence or financial*

aptitude. Over one-third of directors felt that poor presentation skills had hindered their career. Research from the Aziz Corporation, originally published in *Industrial and Commercial Training*, volume 30, number 6.

81 *You increase your value by 50% if you can present.* Warren Buffett quote about the importance of public speaking from his presentation to Columbia University business students in 2009, as reported by Carmine Gallo in "Billionaire Warren Buffett Says This 1 Skill Will Boost Your Career Value by 50%," on Inc.com, 2017. Fact that Mr. Buffett dropped out of his first attempt at a speaking course is from the same article.

81 *Fashionistas agree about importance of public speaking.* From an article in *Glamour Magazine*, "The #1 Work Skill You Need," by Jennifer Breheny Wallace, published November 2015.

81 *Speaking skill is part of one's brand.* Roger McNamee quote from Jerry Weissman, author of *Presenting to Win: The Art of Telling Your Story*, Financial Times Press, 2010. While focused on IPO presentations, this is a terrific book on presenting with broad application, particularly as to using graphics.

82 *Studies suggest more than 70% of the adult population fears public speaking.* From www.ispeak.com, quoting Virginia Richmond and James McCroskey, *Communication Apprehension, Avoidance and Effectiveness*, 1985.

82 *Great speakers make their presentations look effortless, but they are anything but.* Even Samuel Clemens (Mark Twain) said, "It usually takes me more than three weeks to prepare a good impromptu speech."

83 *Public speaking is a prerequisite to an executive position.* Quote from Fortune 500 executive by Brad Holst from Mandel.com blog, "Do Presentation Skills Matter?," January 2, 2014.

89 *Train is to car, as car is to a can of Coke.* From an article by Rich Melvin entitled "What a Train, Auto, Lawn Tractor, and Pop Can Have in Common?" *O Gauge Railroading*, October–November 2006.

91 *Choose a simple and readable font.* News from the *Onion*—Garamond just swept the Fontys!

107 *Don't "water the weed" by repeating ugly buzzwords.* This expression from Arch Lustberg, presentations coach to business and political

leaders (and former stand-up comedian). Arch's works include *How to Sell Yourself,* Career Press, 2002.

108 *Always ensuring an audience benefit will make you "famous by Friday."* Speaking of which, "Famous by Friday" was for some time the working title of this book. Nick prevailed to change the title. He argued that today's young professional is not seeking to be famous, but to make a difference.

Chapter 4: Pitch

113 *Opening quote.* In 1968 Shirley Chisholm became the first African-American woman elected to Congress. Quote thought to be from her 1972 presidential campaign. Another of our Chisholm favorites: "If they don't give you a seat at the table, bring a folding chair."

116 *Study about importance of non-sales selling.* From Daniel Pink, *To Sell is Human,* Riverhead Books, 2012.

116 *NPR interview with Tom Wolfe about importance of rhetorical skills.* Mr. Wolfe's remarks are based on recollection, and notes made at the time, after listening to his interview while driving. We have been unable to find the transcript. Speaking of rhetoric, check out Jay Heinrich's book *Thank You for Arguing,* Three Rivers Press, 2007. A fun read that translates ancient rhetoric into modern-day usage. Per Mr. Heinrich, rhetoric was once the basis of a liberal arts education until it changed to classic literature.

116 *Job interviewers may ask about your ideas and how they were received.* ADP Small Business Guidebook, "How to Start a Business."

129 *One of the strongest signs of intelligence is looking at those to whom you are speaking.* From an article by Sue Shellenbarger in the *Wall Street Journal,* "How to Look Smarter," January 16, 2015, quoting Nora Murphy, a professor at Loyola Marymount University in Los Angeles, who has conducted multiple studies on the topic.

130 *Don't debate what the facts are, but debate what the facts mean.* This wise counsel comes from Ernest M. "Bud" Miller, who rose from CFO, to COO, to CEO of Arvida Company.

134 *Calvin's plastic binder ploy.* See Bill Watterson, *Calvin and Hobbes,* cartoon published on Oct. 31, 1989.

135 *Sell people what they want to buy.* Quote from Mark McCormack, *What They Don't Teach You at Harvard Business School*, Bantam, 1984.

Chapter 5: Lead

143 *Opening quote.* Sheryl Sandberg quote from a story by Cynthia McFadden and Jake Whitman, "Sheryl Sandberg Launches 'Ban Bossy' Campaign to Empower Girls to Lead," ABC News, March 10, 2010.

146 *Team members want autonomy, mastery, and purpose.* See, e.g., Daniel Pink, *Drive*, Riverhead Books, 2009.

146 *To be an effective leader you need not follow rules of leadership.* As we write, an online search of "rules of leadership" takes .48 seconds and reveals "about 595,000,000 results." That's a lot for a new leader to sift through. And there is seeming disagreement not only on the rules, but on the number of rules one must follow, as we found book titles proclaiming 1, 5, 6, 7, 10, 11, 25, 26, 29, 42, 50, 51, and 417 rules. The one rule? "No assholes." See Robert Sutton, *The No Asshole Rule*, 2007.

146 *To be an effective leader you need not adopt a certain style of leadership.* Apparently, leaders must simultaneously be authoritarian, democratic, empathetic, laissez-faire, Machiavellian, paternalistic, servant-like, transactional, transformational, walk-around, and Zen. A tall ask of one person!

146 *To be an effective leader you need not examine the lives of historical figures for leadership lessons.* Books tell us how to lead based on the lives of, among others, Abe Lincoln, Attila the Hun, Cleopatra, Crazy Horse, Genghis Khan, George Washington, Jesus, Robert E. Lee, Machiavelli, Margaret Thatcher, Moses, Mother Theresa, Napoleon, Solomon, Thomas Jefferson, and Ulysses Grant. Be sure to pick up the "box set" of leadership lessons from the lives of "Action" Jackson, Alan Jackson, Andrew Jackson, Jesse Jackson, Luscious Jackson, Michael Jackson, Peter Jackson, Phil Jackson, Reggie Jackson, Samuel L. Jackson, "Shoeless" Joe Jackson, and T. J. Stonewall Jackson.

146 *To be an effective leader you need not lead the way the person before you did.* Effective leaders fit no mold. Some are introverted, others extroverted. Some are more involved and directive, others less so. Some have a bias towards action, others are more deliberate. Some are understanding and tolerant, others demanding and impatient. Some

solicit input and feedback, others don't. All are better at some things than others.

148 *Culture eats strategy for breakfast.* This quote is widely attributed to Peter Drucker but there is some doubt as to its originator. Some attribute it to Mark Fields (later CEO of Ford) in 2006. If interested, search "culture eats strategy for breakfast" and find the article on Quote Investigator. Others have gone even further and said, "Culture eats strategy for lunch." Our research has yet to uncover anyone so bold as to speak to dinner.

149 *Example is what matters in influencing others.* Quote from *Albert Schweitzer: Thoughts for Our Times*, Mount Vernon, N.Y.: Peter Pauper Press, 1975.

150 *No one has ever met my expectations.* Quote from Fortune 500 executive from Stanley Bing, *What Would Machiavelli Do?*, Harper Business, 2004.

152 *The universal need to be appreciated.* William James was a quote machine of pithy thoughts and observations. He went through some challenging times in his career—almost committing suicide—before becoming perhaps America's most influential psychologist.

154 *"Have I got your attention now?"* From movie, *Glengarry Glen Ross*, New Line Cinema, 1992. Based on the play by David Mamet.

155 *The best leaders have a sense of humor.* From Daniel Pink, *A Whole New Mind*, Riverhead Books, 2006.

158 *Delegate authority and get out of the way.* Ronald Reagan quote from the Reagan.com official blog.

160 *Get the planes out on time.* Alaska Airlines COO Ben Minicucci quote as reported by Scott McCartney in the *Wall Street Journal*, "The Airline That Loses Bags, Cancels Flights," January 5, 2012. The airline established some fifty checkpoints for each flight (e.g. 90% of passengers to be boarded within ten minutes of departure, cargo door to be opened within three minutes of arrival, first bag to be placed on conveyor within fifteen minutes of arrival). No standard was set for dealing with annoying passengers who try to board before their section is called, or who hog bin space with over-sized wheelies.

162 *No changes to be made to Mickey's costume.* Michael Eisner directive from Thomas Leonard, *The 28 Laws of Attraction*, Nightingale-Conant, 2002.

162 *Ask questions even at risk of appearing stupid.* Jack Welch quote as reported in *Forbes*, "Thoughts on Leadership," May 31, 2018.

163 *Ben Franklin decision-making method.* Ben outlined his method in a letter to Joseph Priestley, September 19, 1772.

164 *Deliberator example.* From article by Timothy W. Smith, "Just Another Season in Hot Seat for Fontes," *New York Times*, August 14, 1996.

164 *Decider example and driver who didn't bother to park.* No reason to name names here, so please Google it if you want to learn the details of either.

168 *"Mankind was my business."* From Charles Dickens, *A Christmas Carol*, first published by Chapel & Hall in London, 1843.

171 *Difficult conversations.* For more on having difficult conversations, both inside and outside work, check out Susan Scott, *Fierce Conversations*, Berkley Books, 2002.

Chapter 6: Advocate

177 *Opening song lyric.* From Rolling Stones, "You Can't Always Get What You Want," written by Mick Jagger and Keith Richards, from the band's 1969 album *Let It Bleed*.

179 *"In life you don't get what you deserve, you get what you negotiate."* So says Dr. Chester Karrass, who offers a seminar on negotiation. I took it early in my career (Bob), and it's terrific. See www.karrass.com.

180 *"If you don't go after what you want, you'll never have it."* Nora Roberts has written more than 225 novels.

180 *Complaining summer interns who were fired.* From an article on Yahoo style.com by Lauren Tuck, "Interns Get Fired *en masse* after Protesting Dress Code at Work," July 1, 2016.

184 *People with higher aspiration levels get better negotiation outcomes.* See Chester Karrass, *Give & Take: The Complete Guide to Negotiating Strategy and Tactics*, 1974.

187 *A study of five thousand managers and employees found that the highest-ranked performers mastered the art of "selectivity."* From an article by Morten T. Hansen in the *Wall Street Journal* entitled, "The Key to

Success: Doing Less," published Saturday–Sunday, January 13–14, 2018.

188 *Some 43% of young workers are poised to quit within two years.* From an article by Sue Shellenbarger in the *Wall Street Journal*, "The Smart Way to Switch Jobs Quickly," June 27, 2018. Shellenbarger references a Deloitte 2018 survey of over ten thousand millennials.

191 *"When someone's got an issue with me, I like them to tell me so I can fix it."* Mike Babcock quote from an article in the *Detroit News*, "Wings' Babcock Drives Players to Succeed with One Priority: Winning," Friday, May 31, 2013.

191 *Almost 60% of office workers say their reviews have "no impact on the way they approached their work."* From an article by Elizabeth Dunn on Entrepreneur.com, "Performance Anxiety," May 2018.

193 *Young Professionals on average make 20% less than their parents did at the same age.* "Millennials Earn 20% Less Than Boomers—Not as Important as You Might Think," Forbes.com, January 14, 2017.

193 *Online compensation information databases.* As always when we point you to the internet, the most we can do is promise that these websites are active as of the time of this book's writing.

195 *Employees between the ages of twenty-one and thirty-eight are changing jobs three times more than other workers.* From a 2016 Gallup study of two million people, as reported in an article by Sue Shellenbarger in the *Wall Street Journal*, "The Smart Way to Switch Jobs Quickly," June 27, 2018. Some data suggests millennials will have approximately eleven jobs between the ages of eighteen and forty-two. See Carl Bialik, "Seven Careers in a Lifetime? Think Twice . . ." *Wall Street Journal*, September 4, 2010. Another source suggests you can expect to work for fifteen to twenty employers over your career. See James Citrin, *The Career Playbook*, CrownBusiness.com, 2015. That work today for young professionals is more transitory than ever seems beyond dispute.

Chapter 7: Transform

209 *Opening quote.* Few would dispute that Serena Williams is the greatest women's professional tennis player of all time. She has been ranked world #1 in singles on eight separate occasions between 2002 and 2017. When her ranking falls because she misses time due to injury,

or, more recently, to give birth to her daughter, when she returns her peers always consider her #1 regardless of her ranking.

213 *Success means feeling good about where you are.* No surprise, the ancient Greeks thought a lot about success and happiness (*eudaimonia*). Aristotle advises that "nothing in excess" is key to living a virtuous live. See Edith Hall, *Aristotle's Way: How Ancient Wisdom Can Change Your Life*, Penguin Press, 2018.

216 *Act as if you have confidence.* William James taught the "as if" technique: "If you want confidence, act as if you already have it."

218 *"We are confronted with the fierce urgency of now."* From a speech about the Vietnam War delivered by Dr. Martin Luther King Jr., April 1967.

221 *Leading executive recruiter looks for candidates with intellectual curiosity.* From an email to clients from Bob Sherrill of Sockwell Partners, "Traits of Successful Leaders," June 3, 2010.

221 *German composer's annual performance review.* From *The Grove Dictionary of Music and Musicians*, first published in 1904. Pachelbel not only had to perform for thirty minutes, but to do so using all the resources of the organ in "delightful and euphonious harmony." Music historians speculate that tiring of this annual nonsense, and perhaps having consumed too much Jägermeister, he cooked up the intro to *In-A-Gadda-Da-Vida*, later appropriated by Iron Butterfly.

223 *Ithaka.* From *C. P. Cavafy: Collected Poems*, translated from Greek by Edmund Keeley and Philip Sherrard. Published by Princeton University Press. Copyright © 1972 by Edmund Keeley and Philip Sherrard. *Ithaka* appears in *Look Out Above!* with the generous permission of Princeton University Press.

Acknowledgments

The Team

Mentors

Lead: Jules Epstein, Consulting ThreeSixty, Taos, New Mexico
Plus: Karen Bluestein, Cary Communications, Cary,
North Carolina

Editors

Lead: Sharon Broll, Broll Editorial, Byfield, Massachusetts
Plus: Vicki Russell, former writing professor, Duke University,
Durham, North Carolina
Plus: Gibbs Slater, former high school English teacher, Belmont
High, Belmont, Massachusetts
Copy: Fred Kameny, Chapel Hill, North Carolina
Proof: Penelope Cray, Shelburne, Vermont

Subject Matter Experts

Contribute: Gwyneth Cote, Bill Krebs, Jim Shaffner
Write: Dirk Herrman, Vicki Russell, Gibbs Slater
Present: Chris Gilmore, Steve Lefkovits
Pitch: Dirk Herrman
Lead: Gwyneth Cote, Jim Shaffner
Advocate: Will Elam
Transform: Gibbs Slater
Young Professional: Megan Horey

Look Out Above!

Book Designer

 Chris Crochetière, BW&A Books, Oxford, North Carolina

Cover Designer

 Jules Epstein, Consulting ThreeSixty, Taos, New Mexico

Caricature Artist

 JP "Jape" Trostle, Durham, North Carolina

Photographer

 Alex Treml, Alex Treml Photography, Durham, North Carolina

Website Designer

 The TheeDigital team, Raleigh, North Carolina

Support

 Tech: David Alexander, Chapel Hill Tech, Chapel Hill,
 North Carolina
 Plus: The UPS Store team, Meadowmont, Chapel Hill,
 North Carolina

Nick Thank-yous

 Stephanie Kelly for her unfailing support and encouragement, Moose the bulldog for his loyal companionship, and the English Department at the University of Georgia for teaching me how to write.

Bob Thank-yous

 Jane McKee, my lovely, talented, and supportive wife, my undergrad and MBA students at UNC and Duke, who challenge me, and the men and women, past and present, of Trammell Crow Residential, AvalonBay Communities, and Bell Partners, who taught me so much, and were so much fun.

Thank you for reading *Look Out Above!*

Now, please:

• Visit our website at *lookoutabove.com* for more

• Recommend *Look Out Above!* to a friend (or three!)

• Leave an Amazon review

About the Authors

Nick Slater is a borderline Millennial—young enough to be on Instagram but old enough to have suffered the indignity of attending high school without a cell phone. An attorney/entrepreneur/writer, Nick was inspired to participate in this book project after witnessing many of his talented, success-driven friends struggle to find their "professional place" following a devastating recession. As a young professional, Nick is well-positioned to speak to the many challenges faced by the target audience of *Look Out Above!* After all, he's experienced those challenges first-hand.

Nick is a graduate of the University of Georgia and holds a law degree from the University of North Carolina at Chapel Hill. He is an avid tennis player and outdoorsman, and currently lives in London, England, with his bulldog Frank.

Bob Slater is a former trial lawyer with 25 years of executive management in commercial real estate development, management, and investment. He helped build two national real estate companies—AvalonBay Communities (NYSE symbol AVB), a real estate investment trust now among the S&P 500; and Bell Partners, one of the nation's largest privately-owned apartment companies. Bob has also taught undergraduate and MBA students for more than ten years at the University of North Carolina's Kenan-Flagler School of Business and, recently, MBA students at Duke University's Fuqua School of Business. He serves on the Board of Directors of Draper and Kramer, Inc. in Chicago.

Bob is a graduate of Vanderbilt University and the University of Virginia School of Law. He is the father of three sons, including co-author Nick. He lives in Chapel Hill, North Carolina, with his wife Jane and bulldog Winnie.